WEDDING Z

WEDDING Z

How to Reimagine Weddings for the Next Generation

BREANNA DECKER GRANT

NEW DEGREE PRESS

WEDDING Z

How to Reimagine Weddings for the Next Generation

ISBN   978-1-64137-311-1 *Paperback*

         978-1-64137-602-0   *Ebook*

Contents

PART 1

Introduction

Hours before the Hindu wedding, the Priyanka Chopra, now wife of celebrity Nick Jonas, took part in a *haldi* ritual, in which haldi paste is applied to the bride. Haldi paste, made from turmeric, is believed to ward off the evil eye and bring good fortune in Hindu culture. A *chooda* ceremony also occurred, in which the bride was gifted 21 bangle bracelets from family members. [1] She was adorned in the most beautiful, ornate attire costumed to her Indian heritage.

This ceremony is very traditional and a mark of a new bride, bringing good luck, fertility, and prosperity.

And even though these traditions are wildly different than most Western brides are used to, these wedding photos of that specific moment are ones that made every woman flipping through the pages of her favorite gos-

---

1   Kore, Sakshi. 2019. "Priyanka Chopra And Nick Jonas' Unseen Haldi Pictures". *Vogue India*.

sip mag think, "Wow, this is perfect." "I want that in my wedding."

* * *

What do you think of when you think of a wedding? What are the first things that come to mind?

White dress, first dances, wedding cake. Or maybe beautiful flowers, and sentimental vows.

These are common threads in weddings from your parents, grandparents, and beyond. Things that are known to be "timeless" and "traditional."

But are they?

Marrying the love of your life and hosting a wedding has been around long before our Western society put brides in white poufy dresses and served up elaborate cakes. And although the act of finding your life partner and tying the knot may be a timeless principle, the traditions and rituals that many view as "timeless" will soon be replaced with new ideas.

Wedding bells, traditional attire, throwing rice, exchanging rings - these are just a few cliché symbols associated with weddings that we should be prepared to say goodbye to. In fact, perhaps inspired by Priyanka's choices in her photo-ready wedding, I have multiple clients asking if they too might incorporate cultural-aspects into their weddings.

As of 2018, the average age for marriage is 27.6 years for women and 29.5 years for men, but the age is gradually rising. Michael Wood, President of Generational Research says, "Gen Z will likely follow suit with millennials, who have postponed many of the traditional milestones such as buying a home, getting married, and even having children."[2] My personal prediction is that elaborate parties celebrating milestones instead of marriages will soon creep onto the wedding scene. A $298 billion dollar industry that is growing every year, the wedding industry is a force to be reckoned with.[3]

But in order for this industry to keep thriving, it needs to keep up with the demands and ideas of Generation Z.

And because of the unique expectations and values represented by Generation Z, timeless and traditional

2   May, Ashley, and Sean Rossman. 2019. "The Kids Of Gen Z Are Growing Up In A World Far Different Than Their Millennial Predecessors. So, How Does This Affect Their Thoughts On Love?". *Usatoday.Com*.

3   Stevens, Liene. 2019. "2019 State Of The Wedding Industry · Think Splendid®". *Think Splendid®*.

principles which were followed by previous generations are soon to be replaced with modern and unique twists.

* * *

Weddings have grown more and more extravagant in recent years–not just among celebrities or the rich and famous–like pop star Nick Jonas and Indian celebrity and actress Priyanka Chopra had the wedding of the century in 2018. Held in Taj Umaid Bhawan Palace in Jodhpur, India, the venue was adorned with extravagant florals and elaborate decor and looked like it was straight out of a movie. The couple had two wedding ceremonies in one weekend, a Christian ceremony to honor Jonas' faith and a traditional Indian ceremony honoring Chopra's heritage. Every detail was perfectly executed, and it was the perfect blend of their religions, heritage, and cultures telling their unique love story.[4]

At the traditional Western Christian ceremony, the couple initially exchanged vows, with the Indian ceremony following the next day. The number of personal touches and extravagant attire was present in both ceremonies. Throughout the wedding weekend, Jonas and Chopra blended their backgrounds and love story in tangible

---

4   Goldberg, Carrie. 2019. "Everything You Need To Know About Priyanka & Nick's Wedding". *Harper's BAZAAR*

ways, celebrating both of their unique backgrounds and cultures. Priyanka's dress and veil for the traditional western ceremony was extravagant, with a veil that was close to 60 feet long and a custom designed Ralph Lauren dress. The couple exchanged rings, exchanged vows, and celebrated their new union with fireworks.[5]

For the Hindu wedding, Priyanka's attire was equally as gorgeous with elaborate beading and detailing. Jonas arrived at the wedding on the back of a horse and the couple left on the back of an elephant. The couple also participated in rituals such as the *varmala* (or garland) exchange ceremony, invited their guests to an elaborate dinner, and an after-party that took place around midnight.[6]

Extremely extravagant, luxurious, and customized to the couple's unique backgrounds and cultures, this wedding went viral. Every detail flawless, her dress and veil were like nothing seen before, and it was the perfect blend of their individual values telling their unique love story. The wedding received rave reviews from the media and those in the wedding industry, and rightly so.

---

5   Ibid
6   Ibid

What most people saw was a gorgeous wedding that encapsulated this couple's unique story, but what I saw was a massive tidal wave that was poised to change how all of us in the emerging generation will plan and approach our weddings. Generation Z is approaching the workforce, marriageable age, and will hold consumer power, and Gen Z is going to do things their own way. And I am one of them. Born in the late '90s, I am the oldest and in the leading group of Generation Z and am proud that we are stretching boundaries and forging our own path.

* * *

I have loved the magic and the energy of the wedding industry since my freshman year of college. I landed an internship working closely with a certified wedding planner, assisting with all the behind-the-scenes prep and helping her the day of the weddings. For weeks, I was helping her plan and get things ready for our first wedding of the season, but I didn't know what to expect. As we pulled up to the beautiful estate, tucked in the beautiful Blue Ridge Mountains and surrounded by vineyards and rolling hills, I felt a hope rise inside of me.

This hope was because for the first time, I saw the endless possibilities rooted in this industry and believed that my passions and calling could lead to an actual career. This wedding venue was gorgeous and big. It wasn't a dated church or an old meeting hall. It was an elegant estate with cutting-edge renovations, suites to get ready in, views of mountains and wineries. All the staff and vendors present believed in the role they were playing, too. This wasn't a hobby or a side job for them. It was their dream and their career.

Throughout the day, I saw and believed how much my job and the role I played truly mattered. Even as an intern, I was greeting vendors, helping the bride, bridal party, and family get ready, and was responsible for tweaking and styling the details that the bride had worked on for so long. The bride and groom had picked this stunning estate as the location for their destination wedding, so this was the first time I had met them. Every detail had been planned remotely for months, and today their dreams were unfolding before their eyes–partially thanks to me.

Assisting their families as I helped pin on the father's boutonniere and compliment the mother's dress, I was honored and humbled in my role. To some vendors, it was just another wedding on their calendars. But as I saw tears well in the parents' eyes, seeing their little girl as a beautiful bride, I was determined to change my mindset. This was more than just a date I had booked. This was the biggest day of their lives–and I had the privilege to help and serve them.

For the first time I knew deep inside of me– I was making a difference. I truly believed that this could be a legitimate career for me instead of a side job or a hobby. But in order to believe in myself and my vision, I had to see the luxury, beauty, and magic of this industry firsthand. Unfortunately, this is magic that many will never get to understand or experience.

My passion continued to grow, and I started working with more clients and booking more weddings. But one thing I noticed, as I got more involved, is that people in the industry were growing more and more surprised at how much my peers and I wanted to "go off the script." Instead of wanting formal banquet dinners, some of my clients wanted their favorite food truck. I loved their idea, encouraged it, and took it to my company or bosses, who were taken aback and insisted we use their catering company because "that's the way it's always been at this company." I saw other ideas I loved such as pie dessert bars and s'more roasting stations but was met by parents' embarrassed apology: "I'm so sorry we have to deal with these silly desserts." "It's so ridiculous they didn't want a cake." Parents, guests, and the industry at large seemed to be rejecting the new ideas couples from my generation wanted to pursue. But I wasn't sure why. I wanted to learn more.

Because of my first internship, I learned about the certification process and decided to take a leap of faith and become a certified wedding planner at the age of twenty. At the time, I was the youngest student to complete the program and felt empowered by the ideas that were presented. I was surrounded by creative and like-minded people who were identifying and blazing a way for couples who want to "go off the script" and make their own traditions. The passion in the room helped rekindle my passion, and I went back to my wedding field wanting to change the mindset of "it's always been done this way." I felt a calling to pursue my dreams and I felt the same calling to write this book: I want to serve the bride because I am one of you. I am Generation Z. I know our struggles, our mindset, and how we are misunderstood. We are going to make an impact and we are going to change the mantra "it's always been done this way."

The problem with the "it's always been this way" mindset in any capacity is that there is no room for change. As Generation Z is emerging and approaching the workforce and becoming key consumers, they are going to change things drastically. In the U.S. alone, there are 65 million Gen-Zers. By 2020, Generation Z will account for forty percent of all consumers in the U.S. [7]Understanding Gen Z will be critical to companies, including the wedding industry, to succeed in the next decade and beyond. According to Pew Research, Generation Z is "the country's most racially and ethnically diverse generation and is on its way to becoming the best educated generation yet,"[8] and this will certainly be reflected in their values and traditions at their weddings. As a Gen-Zer myself, I know that we want to customize everything, we look for feedback from our trusted network, we crave authentic relationships, and want to personalize our experiences and products. Gen Z is and will be approaching weddings very differently through this lens.

My favorite weddings have been the ones who did things differently; who didn't pursue the traditional. One of my favorite weddings occurred in a beautiful garden on the couple's alma mater campus. It was a smaller, intimate wedding of fewer than one hundred people. They exchanged their vows in an open-air church, with the sun perfectly angling through the stained glass win-

7   Claveria, Kelvin. 2019. "Generation Z Statistics: New Report On The Values, Attitudes, And Behaviors Of The Post-Millennials". *Visioncritical. Com.*

8   "Nearly Half Of Post-Millennials Are Racial Or Ethnic Minorities". 2019. *Pew Research Center'S Social & Demographic Trends Project.*

dows. Their guests enjoyed cocktail hour on a string-light covered patio, with tables scattered through the beautiful garden. Laughter, music, and dancing lingered late into the summer night.

Another bride wowed her guests in a long, green tie-dyed dress. Another couple served a breakfast buffet for their wedding dinner, enjoying their favorite meal with their guests, and celebrating that their first official date, at their favorite breakfast location, led them here to forever.

These couples wildly embraced change, their unique stories, and wanted to do things "non-traditionally." And I believe it highlighted their love stories so much better than any "it's always been done this way" rituals ever could.

Our generation, Gen Z, is unique, talented, and equipped to make an impact. We have experienced things that change our perspective. We were children that grew up through a recession, stretching our creativity and resourcefulness, accepting that activities such as "DIY" are not only fun but also a way of life.[9] Technology

---

9   May, Ashley, and Sean Rossman. 2019. "The Kids Of Gen Z Are Growing Up In A World Far Different Than Their Millennial Predecessors. So, How Does This Affect Their Thoughts On Love?". *Usatoday.Com*.

has always been accessible and is increasing every day, demanding our time and attention and making us choose who and what we give it to. Social media has radically shifted our interactions, self-esteem, and relationships.

Growing up during and after the legalization of gay marriage, Gen Z approaches love, marriage, and equality through a different lens than Gen Y, and even some Millennial counterparts.[10]

The #MeToo movement has shaped our perspective, vocalizing, defending, and empowering each other and learning to speak up.[11] We have also grown up experiencing non-conventional gender roles, with fathers who stay at home and mothers who work 9-5s, or with parents who both have successful side-hustles. We have entrepreneurial spirits, and we want to be unique, authentic, and are constantly living between our online and offline lives. Facing and experiencing these things, and so many more, it is unreasonable to approach us

10   Pew Research. 2019. "About Half Of Gen Zers And Millennials Say Same-Sex Marriage, Interracial Marriage Are Good For Society". *Pew Research Center'S Social & Demographic Trends Project*

11   May, Ashley, and Sean Rossman. 2019. "The Kids Of Gen Z Are Growing Up In A World Far Different Than Their Millennial Predecessors. So, How Does This Affect Their Thoughts On Love?". *Usatoday.Com.*

Gen-Zers like any other generation. We are different–
and we want to be.

I wanted to approach weddings differently. And I want
to be the difference. As times change and our generation
develops, I want to not only embrace these trends, but
also create new ones. I want to build vision, grow and
develop in this career, and be an advocate for my generation in this traditional industry. Why not push against
traditions, embrace you and your partner's unique story,
and plan a wedding that highlights your unique interests, talents, and dreams. I want to help you do this, if
you don't know where to start, and I want to empower
and encourage you that your desire for "more" is normal
and should be celebrated.

My theory is that as Generation Z, we are and will be
approaching weddings differently, in all aspects of the
wedding industry. I will discuss insights that will define
how our generation will approach and celebrate our big
day and how you can plan your wedding differently. I
want to help you reimagine your wedding and equip
you with the tools for success.

This book includes stories, insights and tactics,
including:

- Values and mindsets that are very important to Generation Z. Although these also might impact other generations, the lens and unique perspective Gen Z brings to these topics is intriguing, and shapes the way they consume, interact, and engage with the industry.
- Fields like the wedding industry that are implementing new ideas and approaching things differently. They are in-touch with new mindsets, open to change, and are inspiring for brides and wedding entrepreneurs alike.
- An analysis of the behind-the-scenes of wedding professionals, keys to success when combining our entrepreneurial spirit with grit, and practical ways to tweak your business to make it appealing to Gen Z, so it can be viable for years to come.

As Nick and Priyanka are beaming in their wedding photos and we admire the details, what truly shines is their love. As we admire their unique cultures, backgrounds, and traditions they incorporated, what truly inspired me, and I'm sure most of you as well, is their commitment to celebrate the differences and pledge their lives together, rooted in love.

* * *

This book is for brides, grooms, and couples who are planning their wedding and feeling overwhelmed. Whether you are stuck in the conventional mindset, overwhelmed by traditional ways of doing things, or need inspiration to help you do things differently, I hope this inspires and encourages you. I have interviewed professionals, many who are also Gen-Zers, who will give you suggestions and professional advice. I have told stories of times I've succeeded and times I've failed, and will dive into facts, statistics, and insights regarding our Generation and how we do things differently.

This book is also for wedding professionals who are inspired and excited by the changing industry but who also may feel a little overwhelmed or unsure about how to approach this new generation. I am also one of you. I hope the ideas I present and the research I've collected will be the kick-start you need to revamp your business for Gen Z.

I hope in these pages you will find helpful tips, tricks, and stories from professional wedding vendors who can inspire you. They have such wisdom and experience to share that will help you reimagine your big day.

I will also examine insights regarding technology, social media, branding, and marketing and how all these things matter to Gen Z—not only in their everyday lives but especially as they approach weddings.

I hope that you will be inspired as you read these stories and be encouraged and inspired by these resources. So many talented entrepreneurs and business owners have revolutionary ideas that will change the way we as Gen Z will approach weddings. So, stop browsing Pinterest, Instagram, and getting caught up in the comparison game. Instead, learn from these unique ideas that will help you customize your special day and focus on you, your partner, and your unique love story.

Chapter 1

The History of Weddings

Some things it seems have been around forever, and I would like to argue that weddings are one of them. Since the beginning of time, documentation throughout the Bible, the Torah, and ancient literature hold the records of individuals binding their lives together through weddings. Studying these resources, it is apparent, however, that most marriages were more oriented around political gain or commodity rather than love.

In Genesis 29, part of the Torah, we read the story of Jacob, who falls in love with a woman named Rachel. After promising her father his seven years of labor for her hand in marriage, Rachel's father tricks Jacob into marrying his older daughter, Leah and forces Jacob to work seven more years to marry his true love, Rachel.[12]

---

12   *The Holy Bible*. 1986. New York: American Bible Society.

In this case, the Jewish tradition of the eldest daughter marrying first trumps the father's promise, Jacob's work, and true love. This story, like many others in ancient literature, prove that marriage is a transaction, usually agreed upon between two families for financial security and rooted in work and exchanges– not love. And when love *does* enter the picture, it is not honored by families and instead is twisted for manipulation.

Granted, there are elaborate tales of courageous men who chose to go after their true love regardless of societal expectations. Think of your favorite childhood Disney princess, and the hope of "true love" inspired by the prince's loyal pursuit despite her status or circumstances. But regardless of the hope these stories portrayed, for the most part marriage was based on connections, commodity, and financial security-not love.

* * *

The term "wed" originates from an Anglo-Saxon word that refers to the security provided by the groom's family to the bride's family when a betrothal took place.[13] Today, we think of "betrothal" occurring with an engagement ring and on bended knee. However,

---

13   "Online Etymology Dictionary". 2019. *Etymonline.Com.*

this betrothal usually occurred at the time of birth, or shortly after, when parents would promise the children to each other, usually setting the families up for alliance or political gain. The "wed" then guaranteed the future ceremony would occur. Sometimes the children would know each other, sometimes they wouldn't. Then finally, the wedding was the culmination of this betrothal, uniting the bride and groom in marriage. It wasn't fancy, it wasn't romantic. At the end of the day, it was a business transaction.

This mindset of marrying for "convenience" or "commodity" remained popular even into the 19th century of Western society. But finally, things were starting to change. For the first time, couples were truly marrying for *love* and choosing to find a life-partner with whom they wanted to spend forever. So although weddings have been around forever, thankfully the close-minded traditional marriages based on social status and connections are hardly the norm in current Western Society. Couples marry for a variety of reasons, but at the end of the day, they are seeking love and happiness and the desire to be with their partner forever.

* * *

As I examine traditions and norms surrounding Western marriages, it is interesting how even they have evolved. In the 1800s although marriage was for love, the ceremony was extremely small and intimate with nothing fancy. It occurred at the local church, the bride wore the best dress she owned, and they went on about starting their new life together. As social classes became more divided, the upper and middle class soon started hosting more elaborate weddings, hiring professionals to bake the cake and arraign flowers and allowing their daughters to buy a new dress solely for this day. Therefore, some of our favorite westernized wedding traditions were born in the mid-1800s.[14]

As the 1900s rolled around, couples were marrying at a young age with the average age being twenty in the 1940s. The silent generation (those born before 1945) were traditional, shaped by World War I and the Great Depression.[15] They were conservative when it came to marriage, focusing more on their union than the wedding. Next was the era of the baby boomers, ranging from the mid-1940s to 1960s. Boomers are widely associated with "privilege" since many of them grew

14   Village, Waterloo. 2019. "Wedding Traditions Of The 19Th Century | Partyspace New Jersey". *Partyspace.Com.*

15   Lakritz, Talia. 2019. "How Marriage Has Changed From Baby Boomers To Millennials". *Insider.*

up during a period of increasing affluence.[16] This led to a wealthier and overall higher quality of life in general, thus impacting marriages and weddings as well. Timeless traditions, elegant weddings, and the stereotypical American dream were thriving during this period. But as the boomers transitioned into Gen X, culture and society changed, thus changing weddings, relationships, and love.

Social events have a rippling effect on society. The Voting Rights Act of 1965 as well as interracial marriages becoming nationally legalized in 1967 played a key role in marriages and unions for Gen X, and of course generations to come.[17] Born between the mid-60s and '80s, these hippie-loving, all inclusive, feel-good generation of teens carried their own mindsets into their married years. These mindsets varied greatly from their parents, thus paving the way for millennials and beyond. Concepts of living together before marriage and pre-marital relations were common with this generation, also pushing the average age of marriage later, to around twenty-three years old.[18] In regard to weddings, this was the stereotypical "dated" wedding where you think

16 Ibid

17 Head, Tom. 2019. "How Interracial Marriage Laws Have Changed Since The 1600S". *Thoughtco.*

18 Kagan, Julia. 2019. "Generation X – Gen X". *Investopedia.*

of your mom having it in a church or banquet hall with poufy sleeves, giant hair, tacky flowers, and elaborate cake. Weddings were celebrations and were expected to include each one of these components, truly setting the stage for the next generations and putting into play traditions that we still expect to see at weddings. With Gen X defined as "independent, resourceful, self-managing, adaptable, cynical, and pragmatic"[19] it is no surprise that millennials, who have remained in the spotlight, followed.

* * *

The millennials, who were born in the early '80s to mid-90s. Society is intrigued with this generation because they do things differently. As they reached the age of finding a partner and getting married, they waited longer to tie the knot, with the average age of marriage for millennials being twenty-seven years old.[20] They are starting and maintaining relationships online, are willing to live together and keep dating before locking things down, and are more open to intercultural, interracial, and interfaith marriages than generations before them. Thirty-nine percent of millennials married since

---

19   Ibid
20   Hermanson, Marissa. 2019. "How Millennials Are Redefining Marriage". *The Gottman Institute.*

2010 are married to someone of another race, according to Pew Research Center.[21] In contrast, the U.S. Census Bureau reports that in the year 2000, only 2.6 percent of married couples for that year were made up of interracial couples.[22]

Millennials are willing to splurge on things that are meaningful to them, and this includes their weddings. According to *Glamour* in 2015, seventy percent of millennials had a more "lavish" wedding than their parents.[23] And thanks to millennials, the gorgeous decor, beautiful venues, and elaborate dresses made a comeback in a tasteful way. They also reinvented some "timeless expectations" and would exchange their vows under an event tent or on the beach instead of in the church like many of their parents did. And finally, millennials experienced marriage for all people, regardless of their race, color, background, or gender with the legalization of same sex marriage in 2015.[24] Due to this legalization, which was once polarizing to generations before, was

21 Pew Research. 2019. "About Half Of Gen Zers And Millennials Say Same-Sex Marriage, Interracial Marriage Are Good For Society". *Pew Research Center'S Social & Demographic Trends Project.*

22 Office, US. 2019. "2010 Census Shows Interracial And Interethnic Married Couples Grew By 28 Percent Over Decade - 2010 Census - Newsroom - U.S. Census Bureau". *Census.Gov.*

23 Lebowitz, Shana. 2019. "9 Ways Millennials Are Approaching Marriage Differently From Their Parents". *Business Insider.*

24 Supreme Court, US. 2019. "OBERGEFELL V. HODGES". *Supremecourt. Gov.*

becoming widely accepted as millennials were stepping into the spotlight.

The hype around millennials is still here, causing society to overlook the next generation who is already in their twenties and is ready to make a difference. *This is Generation Z.* With the first of them being born in the mid-90s, they approach the world differently. They approach love differently. And through my research and the research of others, they approach weddings differently.

Online wedding resource, "The Knot" interviewed members of Gen Z about their perspective on love, marriage, and weddings, and I believe they summed it up best:

"I want my wedding to reflect my husband's and my own individuality. "We have our own talents, backgrounds, and passions. Music has always been a big part of my life. To me, the act of creating music with someone is as intimate as it gets. I want my wedding to be about the marriage, not the 'show.' So, I think it's important that my husband and I have time during the wedding to ourselves. I want to comfort him if he is nervous and remind him that I love him. I want him to know that I can't wait to spend the rest of my life with him."[25]

---

25   Lee, Esther. 2019. "Exclusive: How Gen Z Views Marriage And Weddings—Nearly 90 Percent Plan To Wed Someday". *The Knot News.*

Gen Z is centered. They have seen through the façade of social media, perfectly staged images, and inauthentic motives. They just want a real and intimate connection, rooted and focused in love. They are truly reimagining the world around them, and I challenge you to open your eyes to our world and reimagine weddings for our generation - Generation Z.

Chapter 2

My "Wedding Planning" Backstory

"Breanna," my mom's voice echoed through the house. "Your career counselor just emailed about setting up another college meeting to nail down your major." My stomach dropped. Because sitting on the couch, as a senior in high school, I didn't know what I wanted to do. I just always knew I wanted to pursue something different. And I wanted to make a difference. But I didn't really know what any of that meant.

I loved to create things, I loved organizing. Talking to and helping people was important to me, as was flexibility of schedule and the ability to self-manage. These ideas and passions were definitely different than the average office job or standard career that colleges presented. Therefore, I was stuck.

Looking through the degree options on college websites my senior year of high school didn't ever spark anything in me. Healthcare...pass, law enforcement...pass, science, math...not my thing. I was always driven and highly academic, so my career counselors and parents were getting frustrated at my apathetic attitude and lack of passion for standard career paths.

Over my high school summers, I volunteered as a camp counselor, helped out with activities at my elementary school and did some tutoring and had the most hands-on experience helping and working with children. Looking through my options again I randomly decided that out of all of them, being a teacher seemed like my best option. I would have the summers off, I'd be able to use my creativity and organizational skills , and would be able to hang out with kids all day and make a difference in their lives. When I looked at it that way, it sounded pretty good. And out of the other options, this seemed to suit me the best. I filled in the box for "Education" on my application and never looked back.

I showed up to my freshman year of college, nervous, excited, and ready to find myself. With a degree in education, I felt good. Then I had to pick a grade level to teach...and again I was stuck. After summers tutoring elementary school kids who I had to pick up after and help them tie their shoes I was over it. So I blindly said, "I guess high-schoolers would be fun." At least they can carry on a conversation and are interested in things.

Next, I had to pick a subject to teach, and again I was stuck. When you're studying to be a high school teacher, the majority of your college classes are in your "cognate," helping you become an expert in the subject you are teaching. Unlike elementary school teachers who have to be experts in all subjects, from history to math to science, high school teachers are only licensed in their specific cognate. Knowing this, the pressure was on to pick a cognate or subject I really was passionate about.

English and literature....no, biology and chemistry...no, math...maybe. Then I stumbled across a subject option called "family & consumer sciences." When I read about the programs that are encompassed in this field, I felt the first spark I had felt in a while. It gave me options to teach classes about interior design, fashion merchandising, event management, parenting and child development, as well as tons of other options. I thought it seemed cool, or at least cooler than math (which was my second best idea) so I went for it. I was enrolled in the "Intro to Family & Consumer Sciences" class and the rest was history.

*　*　*

My passion was sparked: Ignited by the idea that pursuing a professional title in a creative industry was possible. My department was molding young people to be successful creators, designers, community pillars, and being creative, having fun, thinking outside the box and pushing boundaries was necessary to thrive here. All things I loved doing, was good at doing, but could never do in a traditional academic setting. It was perfect.

Or at least I thought everything was perfect until I realized that my degree was still technically in education and that's what I was expected to do. Be a teacher and educate. I looked forward to every time any of my cognate Family and Consumer Sciences classes met and found myself maxing out my credits and adding extra elective hours on top of my cognate hours to take these classes. Sewing classes, interior design, event management, the list goes on. I was also volunteering in our pre-professional club, helping with department-wide events, fashion shows, and eventually became the president of the club. Regardless of the scene, I found myself planning, executing, and helping with events, and I loved it. I had a gift for it and for once I felt like I was thriving and using my talents. I added a minor in business, wanting to learn as much as I could. I was finally passionate about something and felt like I belonged.

Not only was the event industry piquing my interest but also in particular the wedding scene. It was so aesthetic, organized, elegant (some of my favorite things) and seemed to be picking up steam. After being introduced to the event planning environment during my first year of college, I knew I wanted to keep chasing this passion.

Somehow, I landed an awesome internship as a freshman in college with a local wedding planner. Looking back, I am incredibly thankful for Karissa; she poured into me by helping me see that this dream could be a reality and gave me the courage and confidence I needed. She not only gave me experience, the most important thing, but also saw the potential in me that I couldn't see in myself. She mentored me and encouraged me, and I owe my humble beginnings to her. Because of her, I became a Certified Wedding Planner through The Bridal Society during an intensive course in Florida, wanting to follow in her footsteps. I came back into my sophomore year of college ready to crush goals and keep growing in the industry that so nurtured me.

* * *

With this experience and certification under my belt, I had enough credibility to land my first real gig at the age of nineteen at a multi-million dollar, all inclusive, wedding planning empire in my home state of Virginia, all while pursuing my college degree. And although my résumé and credentials and experience all were official, I was still struggling to understand the main vocabulary and wedding planning "lingo" that was tossed around the industry so casually. If we're being honest, I was slightly confused, overwhelmed, and going with the flow, trying to fit in at my first official job. I didn't want to blow it and ruin an amazing opportunity.

"I can't believe that the bride we've been planning with doesn't think she needs a day-of coordinator," the team lead would say in our meetings with frustration. I would nod in agreement, modeling the experienced professionals in the room.

"Can you believe that the recommended vendors on the venue's list weren't at their tasting event this past weekend?" The room would erupt with disbelief. And I would sit there, trying my best to blend in and pick up on the jargon that I was supposed to know. But I was lost.

And so you're not lost too, let me translate this for you. When a wedding venue (the location of the wedding) is getting started or establishing themselves, they strive to get solid, legitimate wedding vendors on their "list" to recommend to brides. Then, they usually host super elaborate events called "tastings" (named for the food couples are "tasting" provided by the recommended catering companies) and give the couple an opportunity to meet and connect with "preferred vendors" in the area that will make their wedding a success. When the venue's "business allies" aka preferred vendors aren't invited to these events, it is quite a "controversy" in the wedding realm because it implies there was a bad relationship, issue, etc... wedding drama 101. And now, can you blame me for being SO confused as a little wedding rookie on my first week on the job? But I digress...

* * *

Being new to the industry, my young age, and having only one-season of true experience labeled me an outsider. I tried my best, and eventually picked up on all these expressions, but it didn't change the fact that I felt overwhelmed and insecure by the nature of an industry that is in a world of its own.

My bosses would get frustrated at client's emails that they felt were "common knowledge" and be equally as frustrated at my emails, for asking questions that they labeled as "common knowledge" for wedding professionals.

My brides and I were both confused and overwhelmed and looking for guidance. As I grew, I learned and excelled, but my empathy for brides remained. If I, as a Certified Wedding Planner, walking into meetings didn't know half of these expressions, how is the average bride, who is probably working a full-time job or finishing up school supposed to understand what is going on? I wanted to do something to help. But what was I, a nineteen-year-old, full time college student, who was majoring in education supposed to do? I didn't know yet; but I knew I had a passion and I wanted to help.

* * *

My first opportunity with my first full-time bride gave me a shot to get my feet wet, learn from this amazing company, and practice helping her with tips and suggestions. This wedding through me curve ball– a twenty-two-person bridal party, the bride and groom being remote, and trying to stretch their budget to make all their dreams come true. Throughout this experience, the passion I had grew. I wanted to give them practical advice on how to cut corners, stretch their budget, and keep their bridal party on track.

But I couldn't undermine my company by telling my bride and groom that the $600 cake they were looking at was not worth the money. Again, I was stuck, but the idea I had was being shaped. This bride and groom are special to me because I worked with them for over a year planning meetings, cake tastings, menu tastings, rehearsal dinners, and more. They taught me lessons and helped me grow, and I was proud of the work and result of their wedding. And in my work with them, I understood the first statement that had my company so outraged: "I can't believe that the bride we've been planning with doesn't think she needs a day-of coordinator," because I served as this couple's complete wedding planner and day-of coordinator. When you, as a planner, are so invested in your client, planning every step along the way with them, it makes sense that you are also serving as the day-of coordinator, keeping everything together and executing their dreams the day of the wedding.

Since then, I have helped friends plan their weddings, given advice, served as a day-of coordinator and full service wedding planner. My senior year of college, I decided to start a freelance wedding planning blog and business, building brand collaborations, writing articles, and helping brides find unique and meaningful inspiration. My heart still remained with those newly engaged brides who are not familiar with the industry and have no idea what these wedding terms mean. My hope was that writing posts about the planning process and giving tips and tricks would not only give me a little more credibility, but also would validate this career field's importance to my friends, family, and ultimately help brides in their journey. This blog continues to grow, but the original post that started this journey is below, which shows my heart for helping brides and hopefully clarifies the differences of these jobs for my readers.

Wedding planners:

Wedding planners help the bride and groom plan the process, details, vendors, and more. They should start working with you as early as possible and are key resources when securing a venue and locking down details in the months leading up to your big day. Key things that your wedding planner should assist you with are...

1. *Timelines: Planners should know the suggested and professional timelines for the months and weeks leading up to the wedding. They will help you know when to book the caterer, secure a venue, and send out the invitations. They will also help you schedule and plan the timelines for your actual wedding day. This includes the length and flow of the ceremony, the formalities of*

the reception, and making sure all of the events fit into the limited number of hours you'll have to enjoy after you say, "I do!"

2. *Vendors: Professional wedding planners should have connections with other wedding vendors including photographers, florists, and DJs. Because of their experience and interaction with vendors at networking events or other weddings, planners are able to recommend vendors who are professional and fit your style. Also, some venues and planners have a "preferred vendors list" for you to choose from. This is not to "limit" you but to instead point you to the very best of the industry.*

3. *Theme: Planners have an eye to create a cohesive feel at your wedding and to put your style, ideas, and dreams into a reality. Share with them your pictures and inspiration so they can understand the theme you are going for. They will be able to select linens, give you centerpiece suggestions, and plan the little, personal details that bring your wedding together. Some planners also offer services where they will completely set up your decor so all you have to do is arrive and enjoy.*

Day-of-Coordinators:

If your planner does a thorough job, a day-of-coordinator should be able to successfully pull off the wedding day with a just proper timeline in hand. It is their job to keep the bridal party on time, interact professionally with the vendors, and be the go-to person for any need or issue that arises. Their two largest responsibilities are to make sure the wedding party gets down the aisle and to make sure that that DJ/ emcee follows the timeline and announces the formalities correctly. If you don't have a day-of-coordinator organizing the details and keeping everyone on track during your wedding day, you will be stressed to the max and not fully present to enjoy your wedding. You do not realize how essential it is to have someone working behind the scenes — and no... your mom or maid-of-honor cannot do this! Let them enjoy your wedding day, too.

I hope this helped you understand the differences between a wedding planner and day of coordinator and that you will choose to include both so you can fully enjoy your wedding! Now, in my professional opinion, you need to hire a certified and professional wedding planner who is with you every step of the way, meaning your wedding planner should ideally double as your day-of coordinator. But as I use these terms in the future pages, refer to this and remember everything we do. And as you continue reading this book and hearing my stories, I hope the following will give you a lens into our world. I know things can be confusing, sometimes overlap, and our job may seem trivial. But remember our main goal is to serve you and help you have the most enjoyable day of your life.

So if you, like me, are overwhelmed with the wedding jargon as you're first starting out, don't panic and let me encourage you. If you are active and passionate about growing your business, find ways to get plugged in and learn. If you are a bride, don't be afraid to ask questions, hire someone who is a professional you can trust, and don't be embarrassed to ask for help. We are here to help you.

But in the process of working with young clients, learning more about the industry, and researching and writing these posts, there was still one realization: *things are changing.* That led me here: researching and writing this book. I'm eager to learn and research about the history of weddings, how things are evolving, the role Gen Z plays, and how wedding professionals can prepare for Generation Z as clients and consumers. My history and my story led me to this moment. And I'm eager to see where it continues to lead.

PART 2

Chapter 3

Who is Gen Z?

If you were to walk onto a college campus today and listen to the students' conversations, learn about their interests, and listen to their dreams, it would be very different from what you would have seen a few years ago. As I write this, the oldest and first of those born f Generation Z, I have seen changes even throughout my four years at university. I might be dating myself here - but when I arrived at college in 2015, I was eager to get plugged in to every opportunity possible. In my cognate's department, I thought I had found my answer: a pre-professional club for students in my department to get connected with professional development opportunities, learn from speakers, and make a difference in our community. I eagerly showed up at the kick-off event after the first week of classes.

I walked into the room and wasn't sure if I was in the right place. As mentioned previously, my department is based in creative industries - interior design, fashion merchandising, event coordination, and more. The room didn't reflect this spirit. It was quiet, filled with about twenty upper classmen, and led by a handful of seniors who were trying their best. I didn't know what to do. But I saw this vision for what this could be, and I kept attending and encouraged my classmates to come with me. By the end of that semester, the attendance was slightly up, and my Gen Z mind was determined that I would make a difference here. Therefore, I filled out an application to be a "officer in training" for the club.

* * *

Gen Z is defined as the demographic cohort that follows millennials with oldest of the generation being born in the mid-1990s and the youngest being born around 2015. Although they tend to get lumped into the "millennial" comments, Gen Z is a wildly different audience with different needs and expectations. And I think that was proven clearly to me on the evening of this kick-off event, led and attended by almost all millennials.

I myself am part of Generation Z, and so are many of the people I interact with on a daily basis. We think differently, we like to challenge the norm, are driven, and are passionate about social issues. Generation Z is going to be one of the largest and most powerful generations with a strong influence on the future of society. And although you might be thinking that my perspective is biased since I am part of this group, let me back up my claims. I promise I will in the following pages.

* * *

Research done by Vision Critical reported that in U.S. alone, there are 65 million members of Generation Z.[26] By 2020, Generation Z will account for forty percent of all consumers in the U.S.[27] We are the generation who grew up not only with technology, but also the reality of school shootings and climate change. But instead of excepting these realities as unchanging, we want to be our own advocates for our future. Although fifty-eight percent of Gen-Zers say they are either somewhat or very worried about the future, they are also willing to step up and do something at the same time.[28] Sixty percent want their jobs to impact the world, twenty-six percent of sixteen to nineteen year olds currently vol-

---

26   Claveria, Kelvin. 2019. "Generation Z Statistics: New Report On The Values, Attitudes, And Behaviors Of The Post-Millennials". *Visioncritical. Com.*

27   Finch, Jeremy. 2019. "What Is Generation Z, And What Does It Want?". *Fast Company.*

28   Schawbel, Dan. 2019. "66 Of The Most Interesting Facts About Generation Z". *Danschawbel.Com.*

unteer, and seventy-six percent are concerned about humanity's impact on the planet, according to research from CMO by Adobe.[29]

I dove into issues and trends regarding Gen Z by listening to Ted Talks and felt empowered and knowledgeable after listening to one by Corey Seemiller. Corey Seemiller is an educator at Wright State University, researcher, and a leading expert on Generation Z.[30] In her engaging Ted Talk, she discussed key trends of Generation Z and educated the audience on how they are different from other generations.

At large, Gen-Zers want to tackle the *root* of the issue, not just help solve short term needs related to the issue.[31] For example, although wanting to give back to their community, they don't just want to volunteer at a food bank. They would rather help solve the issue of world hunger, so food banks don't need to exist. They are skeptical and untrusting, especially seeing and experiencing so much unrest, growing up during or post 9-11 and the Great Recession. Gen Z wants to disrupt current systems, but while doing so provide solutions.[32]

---

29   Ibid
30   Seemiller, Corey. Ted Talk. 2019. *Generation Z: Making A Difference Their Way*. Video.
31   Ibid
32   Ibid

Their entrepreneurial spirit is alive, with over fifty percent saying they want to start their own business.[33] They see their businesses as a way to solve a problem and create a solution, and thus make a difference in the world. They won't sit back and wait for someone else to solve the problem. They are able to solve the problems by themselves and will do it from a completely different perspective.

Now, although I am fascinated by the research related to Gen Z, I was more fascinated about how it related and would continue to relate to the wedding industry. I could see the writing on the wall, and I myself was part of it. I could see transformation bubbling below the surface. I could see myself and my older Gen Z partners wanting to help snowball this energy and transformation. And as a consumer, I demanded transparency, authenticity, creativity, and so many other things from the products or services I consumed. Why would this be any different in the industry that encompasses the most important day of someone's life: their wedding day?

* * *

---

33   Ibid

It was so inspiring to see how the growth of this pre-professional club grew as each class of millennials graduated and each class of Gen Z took their place. As I remained a leader and officer of this club throughout my four years, I had a front row seat to watch this growth. Membership exponentially grew. Freshman were eager to get involved, asking "what service projects were we planning to partner with" before we could even make the announcement. And I am proud to say that my senior year our entire club, comprised of all Gen-Z members, created more community partnerships, more charitable contributions, and more professional growth than the years before.

Now, in no way am I trying to bash millennials, say they are not community minded, or don't care about professional opportunities. I am just saying that the mindsets are different between these generations. Neither is right or wrong. There are just different core values and habits that cause us to interact differently with each other, with our communities, which you will later see explained in the detail chapters.

* * *

I knew I was not alone in my theories and thoughts that the wedding industry is transforming at an exponential rate. The trends are elaborate, weddings are large celebrated events, and the newly engaged and married couples are fueling this industry with their desire to be unique and celebrate their love story. I felt and experienced this energy at nearly every wedding I worked, but never had the statistics to support this feeling and these observations.

Then I discovered ThinkSplendid.Com and Liene Stevens. Liene, the founder and CEO of Think Splendid, is an author, speaker, and behavioral psychology expert helping bridal, retail, and hospitality brands leverage the $298 billion wedding market.[34] Reading her bio and discovering the statistics on her site not only inspired me but also encouraged me that I was on to something. Generation Z was going to transform the wedding market as well. It would only take time.

Liene reports that in 2017, eighty-five percent of global luxury growth was driven by millennials and Gen Z.[35] As an example, in retail, "luxury" relates to high-end, exclusive brands such as Supreme or Louis Vuitton. Luxury means different things to each person, but in the case of weddings, the evolution of the industry is

---

34 Stevens, Liene. 2019. "2019 State Of The Wedding Industry · Think Splendid®". *Think Splendid®*.

35 Ibid

fueled by millennials and Gen-Zers pursuing exclusive venues with a high price tags, custom-made, extravagant wedding dresses, and larger than life decor and flowers. State-of-the-art vendors are also important, and these luxury consumers look for individuals who have *experience,* with fun and charming personalities. And if that isn't enough, Gen Z also looks at the *community* that surrounds these vendors. If the vendors have other clients that the new generation can relate to, they feel a stronger connection.[36] Again, I saw these patterns working all around me in the industry but having this research and statistics to back it up - WOW!

Now, don't go thinking that if you market as "luxury" your business will be booming with Gen-Zers. We members of Gen Z are a tough crowd. First, being technology natives, Generation Z has the ability to look up whatever information they want with a few taps of a touch screen. Therefore, establishing expertise is especially hard with this group. Gen Z has access to Google, entrepreneurial friends, and YouTube where they can figure most things out themselves. This raises the bar for business owners to show that their expertise is trustworthy, and they can show this in the *execution.*

---

36   Ibid

With Generation Z as the consumer, they not only expect the person providing the product or service to *know* things, but also to *do* things flawlessly.[37] Gen-Zers are such go-getters, non-stop workers, and thinkers that they expect at least the same, if not more, from their trusted vendors. All Gen-Zers can research topics, develop knowledge, and figure out how to create something themselves. However, what is most appealing to Gen Z finding a vendor they trust that can *do* something that they cannot. This is what they will pay money for and this is what will make the industry continue to thrive. This expectation has changed the market some but will definitely change it in future years as those born in the mid-2000s will be graduating high school, entering college, the workforce, and eventually getting married.[38]

Stevens also brings out an interesting point about one of the main differences between millennials and Gen-Zers regarding creativity. Obviously, creativity is at the heart of entrepreneurship and the wedding industry and understanding this concept is critical. According to Stevens, "Millennials primarily consider DIY to be a

---

37   Ibid
38   Claveria, Kelvin. 2019. "Generation Z Statistics: New Report On The Values, Attitudes, And Behaviors Of The Post-Millennials". *Visioncritical. Com.*

creative outlet rather than a money-saver whereas Gen Z considers DIY to be a part of their everyday life. For Gen-Z, being creative isn't an outlet for when you need to relieve some stress, it's very much just part of who you are as a person."[39] As millennials are finishing up their time as the target audience for most of the wedding industry, creativity and individualism will rise as Gen Z takes center stage.

* * *

Interested in seeing what experts in the wedding were saying, I turned to wedding giants "The Knot." Managed by XO Group, which is an American media and technology company, The Knot and other resources under XO Group provide content, tools, products and services for couples who were planning weddings, creating a home, and starting a family.[40]

The Knot examined how Gen Z is changing their approach to weddings and presented shocking statistics that surround this generational cohort. Research they collected says ninety percent of this generation plan on getting married someday and eighty-seven percent say

39   Stevens, Liene. 2019. "2019 State Of The Wedding Industry · Think Splendid®". *Think Splendid®*.

40   The Knot. "About Us". 2019. *Theknot.Com*.

they want to make their own traditions.[41] They seek to "put a spin" on everything in their lives and their weddings are not any different. Establishing new traditions or "tweaking" family traditions in some way makes Gen-Zers feel "unique."[42] One member of Gen Z interviewed by the Knot says, "I want my wedding to reflect my husband's and my own individuality of our own talents, backgrounds, and passions."[43]

So, to my Gen Z brides - I want you to celebrate your ideas, unique traditions, and feel empowered to "put a spin" on your wedding. There is no one else who can or will tell your love story. Don't feel stuck to follow traditions; instead be empowered to make your own.

There are also some take-away's for the wedding community. Some facts and statistics about Gen Z have been presented and they are important to accept and understand.

First, marketing to this generation is going to be different and challenging. Vendors need not only to sell

41   Lee, Esther. 2019. "Exclusive: How Gen Z Views Marriage And Weddings—Nearly 90 Percent Plan To Wed Someday". *The Knot News.*

42   Ibid

43   Ibid

themselves, what they know, and their background, *but also sell their expertise and their experience.*

Secondly, this generation wants to be different; they respect individuality and want to highlight this especially in their wedding day. Make your packages and what you offer *unique and customizable.* Don't fall into the mindset (that is so common in this industry) that they are just another client with another date on your calendar. These clients are trusting YOU on the most important day of their lives.

Lastly, I want to end on advice from Liene Stevens as she encourages her audience about the phenomenon of Gen-Z. As a wedding professional, it is your job to "cultivate an inclusive community that authentically cares about something beyond themselves."[44] This looks different for everyone, but it starts with building an inclusive community in a non-exclusive way. Start a movement within your business or your brand that draws the interest of others that they want to be a part of. Make it charitable focused, others focused, or a way to connect your past clients with future clients as resources. Generation Z *loves* the combination of feeling like they

44   Stevens, Liene. 2019. "2019 State Of The Wedding Industry · Think Splendid®". *Think Splendid®.*

are something special while knowing they are making a difference in something bigger than themselves.

This community goes back to *you*, the wedding planner, photographer, or expert vendor. Believe in your worth, your brand, and your expertise. Create and market this inclusive community and invite your newest audience to be a part of it. And if you're coming from a genuine place, watch what happens–I believe it will grow larger than you can imagine.

Chapter 4

Culture, Diversity, & Gen Z

I met with one of my most joyous brides (let's call her Rachel) at our local coffee shop on a rainy Thursday afternoon. Her bright smile and contagious personally instantly lit up the room, and we were so excited to hash out the details of her big day. She grew up in your average middle class family, who classified themselves as belonging to the Christian faith, but her fiancé and his family were Jewish. Of course, the families were very loving and respectful of the other's beliefs, but Rachel was unsure how to combine their backgrounds, religions, and cultures in the best way possible. She was stuck, and I was a little bit too. These were uncharted waters for both of us. We both agreed to do some research, that she would discuss with her fiancé what elements were the most important to him and his family, and we would reconvene.

Culture is part of all our lives.

We experience culture in our families, in the workplace, in our friendships. Culture is defined by Webster's Dictionary as "the customs, arts, social institutions, and achievements of a particular nation, people, or social group."[45] Our culture is our way of life and is what shapes us. When forming a union in marriage, the individuals bring a unique culture, background, and heritage to the relationship. This is part of you and your partner's unique love story, and should be highlighted and celebrated.

Diversity is defined as "showing a great deal of variety"[46] and this is reflected in today's society more than ever. As social norms change and people become more open-minded, our society is becoming more diverse.

* * *

According to research by NPR, Generation Z is officially the most culturally diverse group in all of society[47], with forty-eight percent of Generation Z representing a com-

---

45   "Definition Of CULTURE". 2019. *Merriam-Webster.Com.*
46   "Definition Of DIVERSITY". 2019. *Merriam-Webster.Com.*
47   Lo Wang, Hansi. 2019. "Generation Z Is The Most Racially And Ethnically Diverse Yet". *Npr.Org.*

munity of color, according to Pew Research Center.[48] Growing up in a society where diversity is the norm for Gen Z, it isn't really a value that they celebrate as much as previous generations do. For example, sixty-nine percent of millennials believe "diversity and inclusion" are important values, where only sixty-one percent of Zers do, also reported by Pew Research Center.[49] In no way does this mean that Gen Z doesn't appreciate or respect diversity - instead it reflects that *Gen Z view diversity as the "new normal" and a way of life.* This is marking an overall culture change that will result in the exponential growth of cross-cultural unions and biracial marriages like never before. [50]

In generations past, many cultures had a "stigma" around marrying outside of one's nationality or culture. Author and wedding professional Eleni Gage, former executive editor at *Martha Stewart Weddings* and expert in wedding customs and traditions shares her experience.[51] Growing up in a traditional Greek home, she

---

48   Fry, Richard, and Kim Parker. 2019. "'Post-Millennial' Generation On Track To Be Most Diverse, Best-Educated". *Pew Research Center'S Social & Demographic Trends Project.*

49   Ibid

50   Lo Wang, Hansi. 2019. "Generation Z Is The Most Racially And Ethnically Diverse Yet". *Npr.Org.*

51   Matthews, Christy, and Michelle Martinez. 2019. "#136 Rituals And Traditions With Author Eleni Gage". Podcast. *The Big Wedding Planning Podcast.*

was very familiar with Greek culture and the assumption that she would marry a Greek boy. She shares her family's traditional mindset and heritage that parallels *My Big Fat Greek Wedding* more than she likes to admit. Despite her family's expectations and culture, Eleni shares she actually married a Nigerian man on an island in Greece.[52] Of course, her family loves and welcomes her husband, but that doesn't change both her and her husband's strong ties to traditions and customs from both of their countries. I loved her story and thought it encapsulated Gen Z well. They are open minded, willing to cross cultural boundaries, and think outside their parents' and grandparents' traditional mindsets to truly embrace love.

Culture goes well beyond our ethnicity and includes traditions and rituals introduced by family and culture. Eleni Gage goes on to share ideas from her research regarding traditions, customs and rituals to personalize weddings. Regardless of our backgrounds or traditions, we all have little rituals in our lives - many that we carry over into our weddings.

"There's a lot at stake," Gage explains helping to explore why incorporate cheeky traditions into weddings. "And

---

52   Ibid

no one really knows how anything's going to turn out. Which is why we develop little rituals that we think we can control."[53]

For example, you might have worn your "lucky" socks on a day you had a test or wanted your favorite sports team to win. At weddings, the mindset is the same. Specifically, a tradition at southern weddings is to bury a bottle of bourbon upside-down in order to prevent it from raining. Eleni said she did this at her wedding and immediately felt relieved.[54]

She said, "I felt like I've done what I can to control the weather. Now I'm just going to focus on getting married and have fun."[55]

Generation Z is also very willing and open to adapt cultural values and ideas from a variety of backgrounds, regardless of whether it is their personal heritage or not. For example, think of how many Americans practice yoga but aren't Hindu. Think of it that way when looking for unique wedding cultures to pull into your wedding, Gage explains.[56]

---

53   Ibid
54   Ibid
55   Ibid
56   Ibid

Gage says, "Find an idea that speaks to you. It's not about taking the ritual of another culture and adopting it completely. It's about looking at the parts of it that inspire you and working them into your ceremony."[57]

So many Generation Z weddings are and will continue to be cross-cultural since this is the largest culturally diverse generation in American history.[58] Figuring ways to incorporate custom traditions from each individual's heritage, as well as incorporating personal cultural meanings will help set Gen Z weddings apart.

For Rachel and her fiancé's wedding, having a traditional Jewish *ketubah* is very important. If you are unfamiliar, a ketubah is a Jewish prenuptial agreement. It is considered an integral part of a traditional Jewish marriage, and outlines the rights and responsibilities of the groom in relation to the bride.[59] Obviously, this has evolved over the years from ancient Jewish times until modern day, but the importance and sacredness of the ketubah remains. Rachel and her fiancé, however, chose

57   Matthews, Christy, and Michelle Martinez. 2019. "#136 Rituals And Traditions With Author Eleni Gage". Podcast. *The Big Wedding Planning Podcast.*

58   Lo Wang, Hansi. 2019. "Generation Z Is The Most Racially And Ethnically Diverse Yet". *Npr.Org.*

59   Lamm, Maurice. 2019. "The Jewish Marriage Contract (Ketubah)". *Chabad.Org.*

to customize their ketubah with beautiful illustrations of their pets with the skyline of the city where they met in the distance, framing the words of their commitment and signatures. The perfect combination of personal touches and cultural significance.

* * *

Now, if you and your partner don't have any cool cultural heritage and are feeling left out, don't worry! There are so many fun traditions that can encapsulate you and your story. When looking for flowers for your bouquet and centerpieces, consider using flowers your fiancé gave you on your first date, the same flowers your grandmother carried on her wedding day, or using an array of flowers that represent "love" in different cultures.

For dinner, considering serving a unique food or genre of food that you and your partner ate on your first date together. Or for the dessert options, only provide desserts that are made from family recipes to signify the blending of your past traditions. It doesn't have to be fancy or expensive. It just has to be you!

Do your research and decide on your story and share this with your guests in the program. They will love hearing the symbolism behind your ideas and choices, and it will help give you the customization and cultural significance you seek!

* * *

Dual ceremonies and combining cultures and faith is becoming more and more common as well. Whether backgrounds are Christian, Hindu, Muslim, Buddhist, or anything in between, couples are finding ways to combine their heritage and faith as they join their lives together. Blended ceremonies highlighting two different faiths can be done through different passages of sacred texts being read, different songs or vows being exchanged, or traditional rituals being incorporated. Also, the option of extending the wedding into a weekend event of two different ceremonies or religious rituals would be an excellent way to combine blended cultures and highlight diversity.

Gage also brings up another excellent point to the importance of highlighting you and your spouse's unique heritages and cultures at your wedding. She shares, "It's about letting these people from different aspects of your life into other areas of your life that they don't really know...and your wedding is their chance to enjoy that experience."[60] Through the blending and highlighting of your culture and background, your wedding can really stand out by the things that have chosen that are meaningful to you.

* * *

Another aspect of "diversity" that is very present in the life of Gen-Zers is the legalization and occurrence of same sex marriage. As some millennials and even more Gen Xers and Boomers were taken aback and non-accepting of this change, to Generation Z this is a way of life. Research done by Society by Human Resource Management interviewed Gen-Zers directly and their report was interesting. These young people said, "We don't focus as much on someone's color, religion or sexual orientation as some of our older counterparts might. To us, a diverse population is simply the norm."[61] So instead of focusing *so* much on the couple's cultural background, sexual orientation, and religion, *let's highlight it without stigmatizing it.* Generation Z reports, "What we care about most in other people is honesty, sincerity and competence."[62]

60 Matthews, Christy, and Michelle Martinez. 2019. "#136 Rituals And Traditions With Author Eleni Gage". Podcast. *The Big Wedding Planning Podcast.*

61 Maurer, Roy. 2019. "What HR Should Know About Generation Z". *SHRM.*

62 Ibid

So I believe that at the end of the day, the way for a couple to truly have a unique wedding is not to make it super over the top or more impressive than everyone else's. The key is to truly make it meaningful and personal to you, your fiancé, and your love story. And that is exactly what Rachel and her fiancé did. At our next meeting, she shared the important rituals they wanted to incorporate, such as the ketubah, breaking of the glass, and dietary restrictions. However, we also discussed personalized, couple-specific elements to incorporate. They tied in elements from their first job where they met, their favorite appetizer of fried green tomatoes, and included their pets in their ceremony. These cultural and personal touches are fun and don't have to be complicated. And if you do it in a way that your guests recognize and can share in with you, it will make it even more special and meaningful.

Chapter 5

Gen Z: Sustainability & Community Giving

I climbed into the back of my younger cousin's car and froze for a second at what I saw. In the backseat of her Rav 4 where multiple reusable bags from her favorite local stores, two plastic grocery bags, (one for trash and one for recycling) and some left over supplies from the latest student counsel charity fundraiser she headed up. At the time, she was a senior in high school, about to turn eighteen, and born in the year 2000 – aka a thriving, passionate Gen Z born in the middle of this generation.

I was in the middle of writing and researching for this specific chapter the weekend we hung out - and it hit me dead between the eyes. Our generation, but specifically the mid-aged Gen-Zers in late high school or early college, are so concerned with sustainability, community efforts, giving back, and recycling, it's almost second nature to them. And even though I am Gen Z myself, I was raised with and surrounded by millennials, questioning my choices and decisions that were and are so different. But as we finished our acai bowl from her favorite shop downtown and put the plastic spoon in the recycling bag in her car, it all came together for me. Gen Z, now having more power in numbers with revolutionary ideas, is here to stay.

Gen Z cares because they see other generations turning a blind eye. We know if we don't set the expectation of using reusable totes for our groceries, no one else will. If we don't show the importance of giving back to local organizations, it will soon fizzle out. We know we are the change.

I believe that because Gen Z is so invested in social issues and the status of our future, they will base their consumer habits around the "bigger picture" products and services that connect their mission to giving back to others or the world. A new study titled "2019 Retail and Sustainability Survey" shows how sustainability deeply affects the buying habits of Generation Z.

According to this study, more than two-thirds of Generation Z respondents consider sustainability when making a purchase and are willing to pay more for sustainable products.[63] Classified as the most conscientious buyers, sixty-eight percent of Gen Z have made an eco-friendly purchase related to sustainability in some capacity this past year.[64] The study continues to report that "Gen Z ranks ethical business/manufacturing as one of its top factors when purchasing" while the rest of the general public in other generations is more concerned about product price and availability.[65] Additionally, "more than fifty percent of Gen Z would be willing to pay more for a sustainable product" because they are forward-sighted and are able to see how their consumer choices are affecting and will continue to affect their future.[66]

Furthermore, research done by DoSomething Strategic and presented by Forbes, shows that "engaging around good causes is a great way for companies to connect with Gen Z."[67] For example, seventy-six percent of young people said they have purchased (fifty-three percent) or would consider purchasing (twenty-three

63 "CGS Survey Reveals 'Sustainability' Is Driving Demand And Customer Loyalty". 2019. *CGS*.

64 Ibid

65 Ibid

66 Ibid

67 Hessekiel, David. 2019. "Engaging Gen Z In Your Social Impact Efforts". *Forbes.Com*.

percent) a brand/product to show support for the issues the brand supported.[68]

Perhaps even more importantly, sixty-seven percdent of total Gen Z consumers have stopped purchasing (forty percent) or would consider not purchasing (twenty-seven percent) a product if the company stood for something or behaved in a way that didn't align with their values. *Forbes* magazine did a segment with Beth Gerstein, the cofounder and CEO of Brilliant Earth, which is an ethically sourced jewelry company. Her input is that both millennials and Gen-Zers put a lot of emphasis on how and where products are sourced and make brand decision based on personal values, increasing social responsibility. Gerstein says, "We believe Gen Z will follow suit with this growing consumer segment."

* * *

Picking up the sturdy cloth tote, I asked my cousin, "Why do you have all these in here and what do you use them for?" I personally had a Trader Joe's tote sitting in my garage for when I needed to make a grocery run, but her parents did most of the grocery shopping. She laughed and replied, "I never know when my friends and

---

68   Ibid

I are going to want to go shopping after school or on the weekend. And we definitely aren't getting a different shopping bag at every store. This way I'm prepared."

Generation Z is also statistically more concerned with social issues such as climate change, equality, and sustainability more than any other generation.[69] Pew Research Center highlights that Gen Z is the most racially and ethnically diverse generation and is keyed into issues such as global warming and agree that diversity is good for society.[70] When talking to veteran wedding planner and industry leader, Laurie Hartwell, she also noticed these changes in Gen Z, specifically reflected in her daughter and her friends, who are members of Generation Z. Laurie comments, "Zs care about the environment; they care about making sure that the oceans are clean and care about climate change, and they are a more involved generation in making sure that things are organic and clean. So, I feel like we're going to see weddings heading that direction."

The bottom line: *sustainability and community giving are driving demand and customer loyalty for Generation Z con-*

---

69   Ibid

70   Fry, Richard, and Kim Parker. 2019. "'Post-Millennial' Generation On Track To Be Most Diverse, Best-Educated". *Pew Research Center'S Social & Demographic Trends Project.*

sumers in every sector. Therefore, I believe this will also impact how they interact and consume in the wedding industry as well.

* * *

Regardless of how sustainability minded you may be, the sad reality is that there is a lot of waste regarding the industry. Decor gets purchased for a one day usage, food gets thrown away, and tons of energy and electricity is used to support a large venue, high guest count, and elaborate sound system. When considering hosting an eco-friendly, sustainable wedding, there are several factors to consider such as location, decor, and waste.

Outdoor locations are not only becoming more and more trendy but are also an eco-friendly option. Vineyards, farms, or upscale campgrounds can be a great option that not only tells a couple's unique love story but is set in a beautiful location. For example, a couple I worked with just got married at a state park in the beautiful Virginia mountains. They both worked there and feel in love there over the summer and wanted to start the new chapter of their love story where it first began.

They also took a very eco-friendly approach to this location, using natural greenery as decor, candles and string lights as their lighting, and rented a portable AUX system that required no on-site electricity. For food, they hired one of their favorite food trucks that served everything on recycled plates and had recycling bins readily available. This is one of my favorite weddings and was done for a fraction of the cost while being extremely sustainable and earth friendly.

Another way to be sustainability minded is to lean into the eclectic vintage trend that is becoming more and more popular. Start by scouring thrift stores for perfect up-cycled decor. Look for a variety of candlesticks, vases, mirrors, and frames to add the finishing touches. Also consider vintage jewelry, rings, or dresses with sentimental value that can be sustainably sourced. Also, lean into the season you are getting married by using the fresh produce, and blooming flowers that are all around locally instead of shipping in items from other regions. Thrifting eclectic plates or using a variety of family china instead of plastic plates or only used LED string lights for reception lighting are little changes that will not only make your wedding stand apart but also do so in an eco-friendly way. You're getting the best of both worlds when locally-sourced, sustainable products are also more budget friendly.

* * *

Putting my bag in the trunk of my cousin's car, there was another box of supplies and T-shirts for a charity event her friends were sponsoring. She explained that her friends teamed up with the high-school student council to partner with local children's hospitals to raise money for children undergoing chemotherapy. This wasn't just one high schooler seeking change but an entire class and student council united in their mindset of giving back. These are their values, as Gen Z.

Another mindset Gen Z is passionate about is the concept of "community giving." Also referred to as corporate giving, it refers to social and philanthropic initiatives launched by a company or group.[71] For example, this would include making donations to nonprofit organizations in order to support and advocate a cause. Popular companies that do this are Toms shoes or Warby Parker glasses that, according to their websites, donate one pair of shoes or glasses respectively to a person in need. Other popular companies such as "Love Your Melon" donate percentages of their proceeds to individuals fighting cancer. Young millennials and older Gen-Zers are rallying around these companies, not only for their trendy products, but also have peace of mind knowing that the companies they are supporting and

---

71   Doan, Dana. 2019. "Community Philanthropy | Learning To Give". *Learningtogive.Org.*

going toward a good causes and that they are able to help others through their purchases.

A similar mindset can be taken in approach to the wedding industry, although it might need to be done a little differently for Generation Z to get on board. Instead of a wedding vendor (let's say a florist) simply saying "XX% of my proceeds will be donated to hungry children in third world countries" Gen Z consumers are going to seek more *connections* and *authenticity*. Instead, if a florist said "XX% of proceeds are going to "save the bees" this connection makes more sense, as the two (flowers and bees) are dependent on each other. Or, better yet, if you gave Gen Z the *option* to decide whether their purchase supported "the bees" or if their left-over flowers were donated to local nursing homes, they would not only love the power of choice, but love the service-minded, philanthropic idea of your company.

Doing other simple things such as asking the caterer to provide separate recycling bins and to donate left-over food to the local shelter are also ways to go a step beyond sustainability and focus on giving to those around you to better the community. The wedding industry is a large community in and of itself. It is made up of so many talented individuals that have influence in their own circles. Coming together to brain-storm ways to bring this creative community into a crossroads with the general community in a service oriented way could really make a difference. And of course, it would attract the Gen Z consumers who are so focused on not only sustainability but also "community giving."

* * *

Now, being a wedding professional myself, I understand that we cannot just always be giving away our products or services - we need to make a living too. However, the "wedding community" is so broad and powerful, I think it would be ignorant not to harness the power of all the vendors working together to make a difference in the industry.

If all of the vendors from each sector teamed up, they could collaborate their products and services to give away a dream wedding. However, instead of doing this to just a random person, it would be so meaningful and impactful to give it to someone in the community in need, nominated by their friends or family. Whether this be a couple who lost everything in a natural disaster, or someone burdened with medical bills, this "dream wedding" could be a practical way for each wedding professional to contribute their talents while participating in a practical aspect of "community giving."

Regardless of the industry, it is so fulfilling to give back to others in some capacity and to know your consumer choices are promoting sustainability. However, I would like to challenge the wedding industry to broaden their perspective and their reach by adapting this mindset as well. Individually and together, wedding professionals have the ability to make a difference in their community—the question is will they choose to be forward-thinkers before it is too late.

And as I now keep my reusable bag in the back of my car and have adapted the "2-bag" approach to sort trash and recyclables while on the go, I smile. Thinking how the influence of a passionate Gen Z impacted my day-to-day living. And I think, with hope, how the impact of this generation on our world in a few short years, can change everything.

Chapter 6

Gen Z: Technology & Media

My alarm goes off on my iPhone and I reach over, half awake, to turn it off. To get my brain awake, I flip on the lamp, grab my phone, and scroll through Instagram. What's better than starting your day by comparing your life to other people on the internet? Kidding, kidding. As I get dressed, I half-heartedly mutter, "Hey Alexa, what's the weather today" and put on the shoes I just ordered online and rush out the door with enough time to make it to my favorite coffee shop. I sync my iPhone to my Bluetooth player in my car, gear up my favorite podcast for my commute, and pay for my coffee with Apple Pay on my phone or my Cash Card (shout-out to that $1 off coffee boost) and am on my way. And these are just a handful of ways I use technology before I'm even awake for an hour or at my job.

We as Generation Z are statistically known as the most technology savvy generation. "Digital natives," we are the individuals who have spent their whole lives centered around technology. Because of this, our expectations about technology, media, and digital experiences are drastically different than older generations and impact how we interact with products and services we consume. According to Marketing Tech, Gen Z engages with 10.6 hours of online content a day, scoring two hours over the average millennial, who spends 8.5 hours a day reading, writing, and engaging in some way with the online world.[72]

Now, before you write this off as Gen Z being "addicted to social media" (like the older generations imply with a snide tone of voice) Gen Z whips out their phones any given second for more than just Snapchat. Instead, Generation Z uses their broad access to media and technology to do research, gain education, and build trust with different brands. Gen Z is big on trust–go figure from the generation whose basic childhood securities have been violated by school shooters, terrorist attacks, financial disasters, and more.

---

72   Hebblethwaite, Colm. 2019. "Gen Z Engaging With 10 Hours Of Online Content A Day". *Marketing Tech News.*

Gen Z looks for security and trusted relationships regardless of the product or service through deep online research. The Center for Generational Kinetics presents that "eighty-five percent of Gen-Zers are trusting of vetted and insured services, such as Uber, and sixty-three percent agree that conducting a background check, having insurance, or some type of "proof" to your name is enough for them to depend on you."[73] But they can research this, validate your claims, and read reviews within a few clicks of a button. The abundance of technology paired with the ability to use it seamlessly is going to change the consumer segment.

This is going to significantly impact the wedding industry as well. This is the generation that is skeptical. And although they trust their Uber driver, this is solely because of the name and legitimacy attached to the company, not the driver himself. As a wedding professional, don't expect them to trust you unless you earn it. They will stalk you on all forms of social media, go deep into the pages of your website, read all the reviews, ask their friends what they think and compare your social media and webpages to someone else's. And still not be certain if they want to trust and hire you for the most important day of their lives.

---

73   Dorsey, Jason. 2019. "Gen Z - Tech Disruption". *Genhq.Com*

I think about myself and the brands that I truly trust and believe in. I was very naive when it came to health and wellness, until my friend brought it to my attention. She said, "Don't you realize all of the chemicals that you're consuming every day because the FDA doesn't really monitor it." This statement caused me to do my own research, stalking websites, comparing statements, and looking at statistics until I found where I stood in regard to health and wellness. I then knew I wanted to make a change and switch out my nutritional products, food, skincare, makeup, and everything in between to products that not only benefited my body, but also the environment. So I searched the web, browsed Instagram, watched YouTube videos, listened to my friends, and found a few brands that stood out to me and ultimately picked one that has excellent branding, a strong community, and adheres to the highest standards.

Although this is a different conversation, the principle I am trying to illustrate remains. I blissfully existed until I was made aware of an issue and need in my life. In the wedding planning world, this occurs when the couple gets engaged, spiraling into a world of excitement that is filled with unknowns, scary situations, and extreme scenarios for which the couple needs answers. Next, the couple is going to do some research, and Gen Z brides are going to have more ways to research than you'd ever expect, sources such as social media, Google, email, website reviews, mutual friends. And this can occur any time of day from any device anywhere in the world.

And you'd better believe that if a wedding professional isn't as tech savvy as their Gen Z client, expectations will not be met. In a digital era, emails are expected to be answered lightning fast, social media is expected to be updated daily, (if not more) and all of this is reflecting on the company and their brand. Generation Z is truly demanding more. And to give their current and future clients a look into their brand, businesses are turning to social media.

* * *

It's no secret that social media is on the rise and Instagram is the platform of choice for personal accounts, small businesses, and large companies alike. According to the 2019 Global Digital Overview, 3.26 million people around the world use their mobile device to access social media, and on average, consumers spend around 2.5 hours a day on social platforms.[74] This is a part of our lifestyles, which can be used strategically to build a strong brand.

---

74   Kemp, Simon. 2019. "Digital 2019: Global Digital Overview — Datareportal – Global Digital Insights". *Datareportal – Global Digital Insights.*

Small businesses are growing in their presence on social media, and this is essential to their success, growth, and legitimacy. However, entrepreneurs in my wedding circles have shared their frustration of trying to cultivate a strong brand and image and the stress and pressure that come along with having to post and create content. Is there a balance to this? Or is this just part of the challenges that come along with being a young entrepreneur, chasing dreams and building your business from the ground up?

I sat down and talked with Deanna Drogan, a social media manager and freelance writer, about the power of social media and her professional opinion about how social media has the power to change any niche industry when used to its full potential. She's worked as the head social media manager for colleges and local businesses and has seen the positives and negatives. She says, "Social media gives companies the opportunity to further their branding through creative content such as images, videos, or even the words they post."

Having a brand in the first place is key, but social media gives companies and small businesses another platform to build their brand and market their values. The key needs to be engagement and when companies are properly using their social media, they are not only building their brand but engaging with potential customers. Drogan reiterates this idea, saying that audience engagement should be a company's number one goal.

Engagement looks different for everyone and can happen in a variety of ways. However, at the time I am writing this, I believe that engagement strategies will make the most of using Instagram stories, giving potential clients, customers, and colleagues a "behind the scenes" look at your business. Where do you sit to answer your emails? What's your favorite coffee shop to meet your clients? Posting frequently, replying to comments, answering messages not only shows your engagement, but allows clients to truly connect and know you care. This shows some transparency and authenticity, but also makes the viewer feel like they are getting an exclusive sneak peek.

Some of my favorite "behind the scenes" posts are as simple as unboxing new products a company ordered that will be available soon or showing a set-up of their workspace where they send out contracts. Another great way to engage and build trust with your audience is to give a few quick tips about a project your business is working on or connect it to a bigger goal. Also consider giveaways, collaborations, or quickly replying to messages or comments on social pages to let current and future clients know your brand goes beyond a perfectly curated Instagram feed and actually cares about customer relationships.

* * *

I talked with entrepreneur and national florist Mary Ellen from Steelcut Flower Co. about how a strong social media presence has impacted her business and her floral design. As Mary Ellen and I chatted, we agreed that the large bulk of a shift in the flower industry away from traditional can be attributed to social media. Whereas in years past, inspiration and resources had to be pulled from local vendors or magazines, Instagram and Pinterest have opened a world of opportunity for vendors and brides a like. Weddings have shifted and grown because of the wealth of resources available to us through a quick web search or following a hashtag. We can connect with people, collaborate, and be inspired by styles without leaving the comfort of our homes. Although social media gets a bad reputation, it truly is inspiring and brings creatives together from all across the world, and has given creators the opportunity for their work to finally be seen and accepted as an art form of self-expression.

However, creating a brand, posting new and creating content, and having strong customer engagement is not always easy. This requires small business owners to constantly be on their A-game. Snapping photos, collaborating with marketing professionals, and keeping a cohesive feed are all important things to help them stand out in this industry. Deanna and I talked about how creating the perfect brand and engagement can sometimes be taken too far.

Instead of posting for fun or because you are inspired, there is the pressure to make sure your images are cohesive and "on-brand," that you post at the best time of the day, and there seems to be no room to make a mistake or have an off-day. Social media comes along with stress and competition, with constant pressure to post new ideas and garner more followers. And regardless of the #communityovercompetition movement and #tuesdaystogether activities that are supposed to build community and rapport between local creatives, it's hard to analyze how accurate this is.

Of course, when push comes to shove, individuals are going to push for and advocate for themselves and their brand. There are positives and negatives to everything in any industry, and the wedding industry is no different. The creativity and freedom that comes along with entrepreneurship is a blessing but presents its own challenges when you are fending for yourself, with no collaborative community or team that you know will have your back.

It may be tempting to build a business empire in isolation and only look out for your brand and business, but I first encourage you to look beyond yourself and think about the creative network of individuals in this industry. You, as one wedding professional, cannot be a jack of all trades. If you are the photographer, you can't be the caterer. And if you're the caterer, you can't be the DJ. In this industry everyone depends on each other not only to find referrals and give honest recommendations, but also to pull off a successful wedding. Each and every individual possesses a strength you lack, which takes humility to admit but will overall benefit the big picture to serve your client well.

And taking it back to Generation Z, they are also able to see how you treat people and how you collaborate by simply taking a peak at your website or social media. And don't think they aren't looking. With over sixty percent of us already being collaborative online[75] this generation is approaching collaboration as a way of life,

75 "Hyperconnected & Collaborative: Gen Z Hits The Workplace". 2019. *Merit Career Development.*

just as much as they expect broad access to technology and social media.

The social media debate about it being good or bad is never-ending, but Drogan says that from her experience, the good outweighs the bad. In my experience, I notice social media negatively impacting my brand and business when I let myself get caught up in comparison. Instead of believing in myself and my brand, I fall into the lies that I need to change myself or my company to look like someone else's. It can also be dangerous when accounts are only posting perfect highlights and are not willing to be honest and vulnerable with challenges they face or the imperfections. We are all human, and the faster the façade is removed, the more real you can be with clients and hopefully establishing more authentic connections.

So, in closing, here are a few of my techniques from research and experience to make the most of social media and to attract your dream clients or your dream wedding vendor:

1. This one should go without saying, but make sure all your social media platforms and website are up to date. Your socials of Instagram, Facebook, Pinterest, and (whatever else becomes popular after this book

is published!) should all be relevant and up-to-date, with live links to your website or blog. These should be clean, organized, and professional as well. Brides, if the vendor you are researching doesn't have a professional feel, look somewhere else.

2. Post. Every. Day. Ok, I'm the first to admit that this is HARD, and I am not great at it either! Finding fresh content can be tough, let alone thinking of a caption, and finding the time every day. My advice? At the beginning of the week, set aside an hour or so to plan out your posts. Find, edit, and favorite pictures you like. Think of some captions and type them in your notes. Use apps such as Later or UNUM to plan out what your Instagram feed will look like or make use of the "post later" option on Facebook. Other creatives are jumping on this idea, so there's bound to be ample podcasts or YouTube content out there to help you with this. When your following sees your posts daily, they think of you and will more likely refer you!

3. Let them see YOU! Not your clients, not your ideas, not your beautifully styled tables or marketing ideas. If you've been around the field of marketing or entrepreneurship for any length of time you've more than likely heard this phrase: "people do business with those they know, like, and trust." If they like your style, think you have great ideas, but have

never seen your face or feel like they don't really "know you," they will have a harder time committing to you and your business. Simple as that.

4. Genuinely engage with those who are following you. If they ask you a question, answer it. If they message you, reply. This is slightly repetitive from up above, but I wholeheartedly believe that successful business owners are reachable and relatable. Which occurs by taking thirty seconds to listen, read, and help those who are asking for it.

5. Give them a call to action or way to ask for more. This one is the hardest for me and has also taken me the longest to implement. Instead of posting about a great wedding you just contributed to, in your caption, end it with a question. Ask them what their favorite wedding trend is or their feedback on an idea. On your stories, don't just post the dates you have available, but add a poll, question box, chat option, or a way for your viewer to react to the content they just engaged in without the luminous direct message.

Now, as you're reading this in the future, I understand that the exact features I mentioned above may likely be obsolete. But my message remains the same. Social media is a powerful marketing and branding tool that gets your name and business out in front of a limitless audience. It gives you the opportunity to connect with consumers and colleagues from all over the country and the world and to be inspired by new ideas that you would otherwise never discover. Setting personal limits, creating a solid community, and refusing to compare yourself with other people are key factors to success. If you know who you are, believe in your business and brand, and are willing to work hard, your business has the power to exponentially grow—all through the power of social media.

Chapter 7

Gen Z: Experience

For years, people have used phrases regarding different events in our lives, saying "chalk it up as experience," or "it was an eye-opening experience" or a "life-changing experience." But as for generations past this was simply as expression. To Generation Z this is a lifestyle. I want to show you how Gen Z holds experiences so highly, even over material things, and how this generation is approaching the thrill of a new experience. This will obviously impact marketing and consuming in every sector, but I want to specifically look at how this will impact the wedding industry and how understanding the crossroad of Gen Z and experience is so important. They want to experience everything.

So what do I mean exactly by Generation Z wanting to experience everything? I personally think, from my own perspective and my Gen Z colleagues - we simply want to experience *life*. As we talk, the thought of sitting in a cubical working a 9 to 5 and living for the weekend is nearly unbearable. We want the freedom to experience the thrill of life every day on our own time. We also want to experience *community*, and within that community, we seek to develop deep and meaningful relationships. And, as haughty as it may sound, we want to feel *special* - like we are the first people (at least out of our circles) experiencing something or doing something for the first time. But now thanks to technology and social media, we are able to see other people all over the globe experiencing new life adventures, which yes, can lead to FOMO (aka the fear of missing out). But nevertheless, we crave the adventures, bookmark the place, and make plans with friends to make this Instagram-worthy experience happen someday for us.

Research done by *INPHANTRY*, a digital experience agency, confirms Gen Z's emphasis on experience. They say, "Although Gen Z craves authentic brand experiences, they also are generally categorized as favoring memories and experiences as opposed to owning material goods."[76] Of course, humans will always consume products in some state or form, but the point is that Gen Z is placing, and will continue to place, a higher value on brands that partner with some type of experience. Think of festivals, art shows, brand-partnership

---

76   "Generation Z Craves Experiential Marketing. Here's Why.". 2019. *INPHANTRY.*

launches, pop-up shops, conferences, or any community events. These are the places Gen Zs will gather in the hopes of experiencing life and community together...and then maybe "consume" or buy something while they are there to remember their time.[77]

So, because Gen Zs are so focused on services and experiences, *INPHANTRY* says that it's up to service companies [that includes the wedding industry!] to prove their commitment to high quality offerings and memorable experiences. So whether you are a Gen Z reader, bride, wedding professional, or anything in between, I want to highlight how these principles relating to experience have been influencing and will continue to shape the wedding industry - and how *your* wedding can be classified (by this picky audience I might add) as a "memorable experience."

Whether you are a photographer, florist, caterer, or anything in between, your services play a key role in offering products or services to the couple in hopes of making their wedding the best day of their lives. First, use the thrill of the experience to book your clients. As mentioned, these Gen Z clients flock to community events where they can be social and see and do some-

---

77   Ibid

thing exciting and different. As a wedding professional, I have experienced success for myself, and seen great success for others at wedding expo events, bridal pop-up shops, and open-houses. Clients from around the area frequent these events in the hope of not only booking vendors, but also, and more importantly experiencing something fun. There are usually giveaways, food, music, and opportunities to be inspired by designs and ideas, as well as, the "Instagram worthy" shot and the opportunity to feel "special."

Another experience is hosting small scale events and workshops, offering limited spots and spoiling the guests who do sign up. This can be done in multiple ways, one of my favorites being where the guests work on making or creating something (that is related to your product or brand.) While mingling, eating, and creating something fun, they are also learning more about you and your company. They then leave with something to remember the experience by...and hopefully remember you too! All while feeling super special and exclusive, building community, and having a fun, creative time.

Now, these same principles can be applied to the actual wedding day, so brides and planners listen up! We've all been to a wedding where you're just kind of sitting there waiting for dinner, awkwardly listening to the toasts, and waiting for the bar to open and the dance floor to get fun. Now don't get me wrong, celebrating and honoring the couple's love and commitment is obviously most important and the reason everyone is gathered. However, sometimes it's the small personal touches that make a wedding unique and memorable for years to come and will really make everyone have the best experience. Here are some ideas I've seen throughout the years or thought up on my own that brides and wedding planners alike can do to make their wedding and overall experience unique, fun, and memorable.

1. Having a unique ceremony set-up is definitely different and has a way of bringing everyone together during the most important part of the day. Instead of having a traditional aisle with two separate sides, try a unique chair set up. For example, put the chairs in a circle or spiral surrounding where you will say "I do" or have two aisles—one to enter down and one to exit. These simple changes are free, unique, and will give all guests a better view. Despite the venue, the number of guests, or time of day, this is something you can do that will make your guests a more intimate part of your day.

2. A themed cocktail hour is becoming a popular trend. This is not only a fun way to keep your guests entertained but also a way to incorporate your wedding

theme and set the tone for the rest of the evening. If you're having an intimate rustic wedding, have interactive stations such as a mini s'mores or gourmet slider stations and hire your favorite bluegrass band. If you're having a large glamorous wedding, set the mood with passed hors d'oeuvres, his and hers cocktails, and a classy jazz ensemble. This is your time to set the tone for the rest of the night— so make it fun and unique!

3. Going along with this, I love the trend of having food trucks at the wedding! You can incorporate this into cocktail hour, as the main dinner course, a reception snack, or even a dessert option. This not only lets your guests learn about your favorite place, but it can serve as an overall entertainment spot for the evening. Whether it is ice cream, coffee, or your favorite taco truck, your guests will love this unique food option and you will love having your favorite food there too.

4. Another food themed idea, alternative to a buffet or plated dinners, is to have food stations set up around the room or venue. This keeps your guests socializing while also experiencing some unique favorites. Popular options include a custom pasta bar, crepe stations, gourmet grilled cheese stations, tossed salad stations, taco stations, and more.

5. Another unique idea I love that creates the "community" experience is having guests stick to a certain color scheme. The aesthetics, theme, and unity that it promotes is beautiful, and it adds no additional costs for the bride and groom! Kindly ask your guests to wear a certain color or stick to a certain theme (ex: please wear a semi-formal dress in any shade of blue). This is especially beautiful at intimate weddings making everyone in photos look cohesive and feel part of the bigger love story.

6. To keep the "community" feeling going, consider setting up interactive stations where you and your guests create lasting memories. For example, instead of simply having guests sign a guest book when they arrive, have them collectively paint a canvas, play games, write down ideas for future baby names, or give date night ideas to the newlyweds. This will keep guests interacting, give them options if they need a break from dancing, and create a memorable experience.

Research done by entrepreneur.com says, "It is often the little details that customers recall even more than the product they purchased or the service they received."[78] Details such as personalization of stationary and cus-

---

78 Barrows, Sydney. 2019. "Six Ways To Create A Memorable Customer Experience". *Entrepreneur.*

tomized thank you notes can go a long way and make a big impression with guests. Consideration and appreciation go a long way when dealing with customers in retail and small businesses, so why wouldn't the same go for wedding guests? Going the extra mile for your guests to ensure that they have the best experience possible shows that you not only appreciate the efforts they made to come, but also want to ensure they have a fun time celebrating with you.

As Gen Z is rising, we as business owners, wedding hosts, and even future brides will truly see that "the devil is in the details." *Harvard Business Review* sums it up best saying, "The experience doesn't begin or end with one function. It's the sum of all touchpoints and interactions that occur throughout a customer's relationship with your brand."[79]

---

79   Barrett, Jana. 2019. "How To Deliver A Great Customer Experience". *Getfeedback Blog.*

Chapter 8

Gen Z & Customization

Next time you're in a trendy restaurant or cafe or are shopping at a local boutique or on an up-and-coming website I challenge you to look for something: I want you to see how many items on the menu or items at the store can be specifically customized.

"Hi, can I please get an iced latte, but with light ice, an extra shot, oat milk, with sugar-free vanilla," you might hear a Gen Z order at their favorite coffee shop. Count the customizations in that order alone. And if for some reason, the coffee shop doesn't offer "oat milk" or "sugar-free vanilla, good luck having that Gen Z be a repeat customer. And if you're anything like my Gen X parents, you'd probably just order a black drip coffee. Shaking your head at how unnecessarily complicated my order was.

I want to show you that Generation Z is a generation that is obsessed with being unique and having a customized experience, which will sooner or later impact the wedding world.

In the past few years, millennials have been the consumers in the cross-hairs, and they started the personalization trend, while putting a high value on luxury products. According to research done by The Campaign Company, "A luxury for millennials is something that demonstrates not wealth and status, but their own uniqueness–their experiences, their ideas, their story. And for Generation Z, this is even more of a focus."[80]

Generation Z is continually in the process of "constructing their own individual identities" while paying no regard to the norms of society.[81] A big influence of the "customization" mindset can be attributed to social media, giving each and every person a platform to have a voice and customize their platform into the image they want to portray. Customization has its roots in uniqueness: *breaking traditions and being yourself.*

Millennials have paved the way for the next generations, writing their own rules and breaking some traditions. Customization is the name of the game, and millennial

80   Kleinschmit, Matt. 2019. "Generation Z Characteristics: 5 Infographics On The Gen Z Lifestyle". *Visioncritical.Com*

81   Ibid

and Gen Z couples want their wedding to be unique and individual. This is in all areas and is as specific as the gifts they are registering for, to the experiences they are providing their guests, and what they are wearing.

* * *

For my own wedding, I emailed the caterer in distress, saying I wanted the food to be *unique and different*. I had a dilemma at the wedding dress shop, totally in love with the dress I was wearing, but wondering if it was *unique* enough or if there was anything, I could do to *customize* it. Luckily, my fiancé avoided this issue and custom-designed my engagement ring. But throughout this process I felt slightly ashamed for being a "diva" and wanting everything "unique" and "customized." I knew it couldn't be just me, right?

Expectations are changing, and instead of being fine with a wedding happening in the same place, with a similar dress as their Facebook friend and serving similar food, Gen Zs are willing to go to drastic measures to ensure they are not reflecting any mainstream ideas or being too similar to any of their friends who are also getting married.

Laurie Hartwell reflects on this saying, "What I find most often is that the industry is transforming by becoming so much more custom. We aren't just doing the same thing over and over and over again, just because that's what the last wedding did...I'd say the vast majority really would like to customize how their wedding is."

The industry is flipping; instead of wanting to do something because "that's how everyone else is doing it" Gen Z wants to do things because no one else is doing it. And the sole way to make sure no one else is doing it is to make it personalized and unique; certainly no one is quite like you.

This can happen in a variety of ways such as providing lawn games and interactive stations, hosting a more casual wedding in the afternoon with themed cocktails, or a "brunch" wedding with teas and fun pastries. Today's couples are shying away from the traditional, are more relaxed, and just want to have fun.

* * *

Forbes reflects on how Gen Z expects personalized experiences because "they have grown up exiting out of pop-up ads and being bombarded by brands at nearly every stage of their day."[82] They also remind us of the daily tailor-made services, such as Spotify playlists, elaborate food and Starbucks drink orders, and email and advertisement preferences, Gen Z has the power to control and customize.[83] Leveraging the power of customized can be a game-changer while planning your wedding, or even for your wedding business or service if channeled correctly.

I wanted to clearly define "customization," "personalization," and "individualization" as they relate to Generation Z.[84]

- **Customization** allows consumers to assemble their own, unique product according to their particular tastes and needs. Think of going to your favorite brand's online website and picking out the exact color combination and style that you want your shoes.
- **Personalization:** Driven by the brand to tailor consumer shopping experiences, the company makes a product "just for you." Think of a bag with your

82 Wertz, Jia. 2019. "How To Win Over Generation Z, Who Hold $44 Billion Of Buying Power". *Forbes.Com.*
83 Ibid
84 Ibid

initials on it or certain health supplements that are designed just for your needs.

- **Individualization:** Driven by consumers, enabling them to individualize and customize their own singular shopping experiences.

As I'm using these words–customization, personalization, individualization–please understand that they mean different things related to consumer and customer relations, but my message is the same: Generation Z seeks a customized world every day and will continue to keep seeking it.

Why? According to a study from the IBM Institute for Business Value, they report that Gen-Zers find value provided at an individualized level[85]. Research done by Robin Nichols presents that these strategies aim to make consumers feel uniquely understood and marketed to as individuals.[86] They also put a high value on self-expression and personal tastes and experiences, while creating the illusion that consumers are being given special treatment and have a *one-on-one relationship with the brand.*[87]

---

85   Glass, Simon, Christopher Wong, David McCarty, and Jane Cheung. 2019. "What Brands Should Know About Generation Z Shoppers". *IBM Institute For Business Value.*

86   Nichols, Robin. 2019. "Customization And Personalization - Marketing For Millennials". *AB Tasty.*

87   Ibid

So because Generation Z has and will continue to have these different expectations as consumers, those providing a product or service may need to readjust their strategies. To Gen Z, being innovative is an expectation, because Gen-Zers are very innovative themselves. As a Gen-Zer myself, I can agree. I look for someone who has high expertise in areas I lack, and if they give me any reason to question their expertise, or I think for even a second I could do something similarly myself; I trust my own creativity.

Those providing products and services to this new generation must be willing to change their mindset to embrace creativity and customization. As Gen Z, we want to be different and put our own spin on things, but don't want it to be *so* different that our peers judge or reject it. As a wedding professional, offering services that can be customized and tailored to each customer is what will set you apart. But doing this while maintaining your brand and your professionalism is what will make you thrive.

As you continue reading, I present some companies who are reimagining their sector of the industry and are transforming the experience for brides and grooms across the country- and the world. But as you read, I encourage you to keep all of Generation Z's expectations in mind such as sustainability, technology, and culture - but especially when it comes to customization. From rings, to dresses, to venues, the companies presented here have stepped outside the industry norm and are making great progress, and I personally believe a large part of their growth is due to their increased acceptance of customization, personalization, and individuality in their sector.

There is only one you and one of your brand. But there is also only one unique consumer behind every sale and every contract. As you read, regardless if you are a consumer or a business owner, I hope you are challenged and inspired. Finding the sweet spot where a unique brand aligns with your unique personality and desires will be the start of something big, regardless of your niche and industry.

PART 3

Chapter 9

Reimagine Registries

Before I was even engaged, I was browsing Pinterest and wedding companies - searching ideas and looking for inspiration. I not only loved the business side of wedding planning, but also loved the creativity that it brought me. As I continued browsing ideas, intriguing graphics from a company called Zola kept crossing my radar. These graphics had wonderful tips and tricks for planning weddings, creating a guest list, hiring vendors, and more. I pinned the idea and moved on, not knowing what impact this company would have on me down the road.

A few months later, one of my boyfriend's best friends sent out his wedding invitation with the words "learn more about our wedding details at Zola.com." I asked my boyfriend if he knew what this was all about since it was his friend's invitation, and like a typical guy, he didn't know much, so I was intrigued. I thought Zola was just a resource for wedding tips and tricks? What "wedding details" did they have on there? I pulled up Zola, typed in the couple's name, and unlocked an online resource that would change how I approached wedding planning.

So let's look at industry leader Zola and how it has taken over this niche, combining technology, wedding planning, wedding registries, and more. Zola is transforming the registry experience by letting couples opt out of the traditional options such as fine china and put things like honeymoon experiences, technology, or charitable donations. Zola is an online wedding registry, wedding planner, and retailer. It is a female led e-commerce company founded in 2013 that allows couples to register for gifts, experiences, and cash funds as well as add gifts from other stores.[88] On their website, Zola elaborates their mission saying, "Zola Weddings is a free suite of wedding planning tools including your wedding website, registry, checklist, and guest list."[89] Next, Zola breaks it down so couples can better understand how to use these resources.

1. First, brides and grooms can create a free wedding website. These are very easy to use and create, with many colors and personalization options. Add details about your love story, information about

---

88 "Zola (Company)". 2019. *En.Wikipedia.Org.*
89 "About Zola Wedding Registries". 2019. *Zola.*

your wedding ceremony and reception, and countless other details that will make wedding planning easier for you and for your guests.

2. Zola prides itself on being a revolutionary registry experience, truly helping couples and the industry at large reimagine the wedding registry experience. Zola says, "With our registry, you can register from our endless collection of gifts, experiences, and funds–plus enjoy benefits like free shipping, group gifting, price matching, choosing when gifts ship, adding gifts from any other store, and more." It really is anything and everything you need all in one place!

3. Zola also includes a very helpful checklist that can be customized based on cultural preferences and religious backgrounds to ensure that every couple can stay on track despite their unique story. You are also able to tweak your own tasks and deadlines. Many of the suggested deadlines align with my professional suggestions as a wedding planner, so this is a helpful resource if you do not have access to a wedding planning professional to help keep your life and tasks in order.

4. Zola also offers a revolutionary guest list tool, which has personally impacted me and many brides! Zola builds your guest list for you; all you have to do is text or email your guests the Zola link. Then they

enter their contact information and Zola collects addresses, addresses invitations, tracks RSVPs and gifts, and lets you communicate with your guests before, during, and after the big day.

Interview with Zola's founder, Shan-Lyn Ma, is so illuminating, shedding light on the inspiration and creativity that has gone into the fast-growing start up. Since creating Zola in 2013 from her Brooklyn living room, Shan-Lyn Ma built her startup into the fastest growing wedding registry in the U.S., valued at more than $220 million and having over 500,000 users.[90] According to Ma, Zola was founded out of personal need. She was at the stage of life where many of her friends were getting married and as she was hunting for the perfect gift to buy them, she was getting frustrated.[91] Ma explains, "I was appalled at how tedious and impersonal the wedding gift shopping experience was."[92] Seeing this as an opportunity, Ma left her corporate job and partnered with friend and former colleague Nobu Nakaguchi to start Zola in the hope of giving couples and guests a better way to reimagine wedding registries.[93]

90   "10 Questions With Shan-Lyn Ma, Founder & CEO At Zola". 2019. *Medium*.

91   Ibid

92   Ibid

93   Ibid

Zola started as simply a revolutionary wedding registry, combining items from many different marketplaces in one online site. Competing with the traditional registry mindset, Ma says they were thinking too narrowly. Her realization was "if we build a lot of valuable tools for free, couples will see how well we work and want to register with us to have everything in one place."[94] With this change in mindset, Zola began offering the services mentioned above: from a free wedding website, guest tracker, planning resources, and more.

So what makes Zola so successful? First, I believe because it is so *tech-centered*, it makes it convenient for everyone. Brides and grooms can build their wedding websites and their registries in their pajamas in their living room instead of having to make a trip to the local home goods store and registering for fine china. It also is very user friendly, recommending ideas for registry essentials and price matching any product. Although the older generation of grandparents and parents that may be mind-boggled at an "online wedding registry" the millennials and Gen-Zers that will be wedding guests at majority of weddings will really appreciate this tech-based registry experience.

---

94   Ibid

Secondly, Zola is growing in popularity due to its high *customization* options, very important to most millennials and even more so to Generation Z brides. From the website style option to the color of the mixer you put on your registry, Zola is giving couples the power to perfectly personalize and customize their wedding experience, starting with the planning process. As mentioned above, the checklist is personalized due to your unique background and culture, ensuring you're always on track in the planning process.

Time is money with this generation, and Zola is the definition of convenient. I personally used their services for my wedding website, along with the guest tracking service through the convenient link that you can send to your guests. Also, adding helpful info to the website, such as local favorite places, accommodation options, travel info, and more is super convenient. That way when it's closer to the time of the wedding and people are asking trivial questions, you can point them to your wedding website.

Zola also taps into millennial and Generation Z's desire to give, letting individuals choose to register for (and therefore donate) to causes from fighting hunger, disaster relief efforts, animal-based charities, and more. These giving options are more far-reaching that just giving the couple another set of cups and can align with the couple's values and lifestyle.

Similar to this option, guests are also able to gift "experiences," which are especially related to the honeymoon. Register for round-trip plane tickets, dinner for two, resorts, or an art collection. This option is truly revolutionary and is especially good for the modern couples whom we will begin seeing more of today. Couples are marrying later in life, and therefore usually have sheet sets, throw pillows, small appliances, and plates, the usual registry items. These unique "cash fund" gift options allow guests to contribute to an experience (check for Gen Z) or a cause about which the two of you are truly passionate.

Some suggestions on the Zola website are a cash fund for a home down-payment, a new dog or new cat fund, or monthly subscription services that would be considered splurges when first starting out. Regardless of the unique cash fund option you choose, Zola is giving couples the option to customize the gifting experience with just a few clicks of a button and making it very in-touch with the younger generations.

So next time you're invited to your college friend's wedding and don't know what to get them, check into Zola for some creative inspiration. And if they aren't registered at Zola yet, you're now equipped with the perfect pep talk to convince them that this is the best option for all things wedding registries.

Chapter 10

Reimagine Photography

It is so encouraging when you find someone who is like-minded. It's like they understand your thoughts, perspective, and heart before you have time to even express yourself, and it is SUCH a good feeling! That's why I am so excited to highlight these two photographers - Hope Taylor from Hope Taylor Photography and Melissa Durham from Ocean & Ridge Photography. They are joining in on this conversation about the evolution of the wedding industry from a photographer's perspective. They are truly helping clients and professionals reimagine their photography business and how much photography can impact the wedding day.

I met both Hope and Melissa through Instagram. It is still so funny to me how an app with little squares has the power to connect people from all careers and walks of life. Hope is a full-time wedding photographer with her headquarters originally in Virginia, but is now located in Charleston, South Carolina. Growing up in Virginia myself, I heard her name every now and again when discussing photographers. She is a photographer for the classic, Southern bride, and specializes in vibrant, full of life images that tell a story. Also based in Virginia but available for travel, Melissa specializes more in elopements and intimate weddings, with images of couples dancing in the mountains or on the coast.

I believe that Hope, Melissa, and so many more photographers are transforming and reimagining the wedding industry through their approach. Photographers are the only vendors whose contribution to the wedding will live long beyond that day, and will live on even beyond the couple themselves. Photography has the power to transcend decades and centuries, telling stories to future generations. Regardless of the style, location, or couple, a photographer is always a key player.

* * *

Photography has changed from formal, stuffy portraits into beautiful artistry that tells a story. With that, photographers have changed their shooting styles, packages, and overall "feel" that they want their images to represent. You may find a tag line on current photographers' websites that read, "capturing your raw and adventurous love." These photographers' photos show candid, intimate moments. These are the moments that Gen Z couples want captured forever, not stiffly posed portraits.

Melissa Durham adds changes she has seen in the photography industry, specifically related to this. She adds that her Gen Z clients, and even earlier clients appreciate emotion and movement in their photos. "They love details, too," Melissa adds, "but they LOVE movement and candid moments; moments full of emotion, passion, and chemistry." Melissa comments that in wedding photography, there has to be a balance. So Melissa says, "As a photographer, I focus on two things when I do portraits: traditional so parents and grandparents don't hate me and then it's ALL movements and emotion and intimacy." Melissa says she will nail down family formals or wedding party formals, for obvious reasons, but then the rest of it is centered around candid and fun moments filled with movement. "We've gone from still photos and poses to moments and living life," Melissa adds. And couples in Generation Z, as well as myself, are definitely drawn to this!

* * *

The "timeline" regarding photography and how photos play out during the day has also changed so much with younger generations. Gen Z is "reimagining" tradition when it comes to seeing each other before the wedding, and this change impacts photographers the most. Millennials introduced the idea of the "first look," which nearly all Gen Z brides are implementing in their wedding day. If you are unfamiliar, the *first look* is when the bride and groom share an intimate moment together and see each other before the official ceremony. This is a time to release some nerves, take some beautiful pictures, and spend some alone time together.

Although this idea is mind-blowing to older generations (my mom, mother-in-law, and grandmothers could hardly believe that we wanted to see each other before the ceremony), Generation Z is accepting it and encouraging the idea. When talking with my clients who are unsure or unfamiliar, I always encourage it as a special moment that results in beautiful images.

Melissa adds her opinion about first looks from a photographer's perspective, admitting that she was even shocked when they first emerged. "I used to think, why would you want to see each other before the wedding?! I was so used to the tradition of the altar, and even used a blusher walking down the aisle at my own wedding in

2006." Now, when I ask Melissa which she prefers, she says that she honestly loves both. "I've made sure to embrace the uniqueness that my couples bring forth. It makes what I do that much more exciting but also keeps me focused on emotion and documentation, rather than just 'knowing the ropes' and it becoming mundane." I love her perspective on this—keeping the couple and their unique story at the center.

* * *

Clients have also changed their photography expectations and perspective with the changing times. The newest generation of brides are overall increasing their budget, and, according to Hope Taylor, are willing to pay more for a quality photographer and cherish the photos forever. Photos outlive the moment, and even the couple and transcend time. Many photographers label their "pricing" tab on their site with the name "investment." Because having gorgeous images you will cherish forever is definitely an investment worth making.

Brides are also more proactive in the planning process and book their vendors, especially photographers, a year or more in advance! This has definitely changed and will continue to be more of something to consider when booking any vendor, but especially wedding photographers. Social media plays a big role in this as well. Photographers can now connect and book clients outside of their immediate region, making their demand greater.

One reason for this regional growth is that photographers have opened their services to the elopement market, targeting the couples who want to keep their weddings small and intimate. I especially think that elopement style weddings are going to be increasingly popular with Generation Z, and it's partially to thank to the open-mindedness of current photographers who embraced this idea. Instead of shying away from intimate weddings, photographers are embracing them, thus helping increase their sales. Instead of being scared of new ideas or trends, truly successful entrepreneurs will run towards them with the mindset of success.

Hope Taylor ended our conversation by sharing some advice—advice she would give to brides looking to hire a wedding photographer. First for the brides, when looking to hire a photographer, make sure you not only LOVE their work, but also LOVE them! Hope says, "Your photographer will spend more time with you on your wedding day than the partner you are marrying, so be sure you get along well with them outside of loving their images!" Beginning first thing in the morning to the end of the day, your wedding photographer will be by your side, celebrating, crying, and smiling with you. If you find someone whose work you love, who you get along with as a person, and who is available on your wedding date, book them FAST!

My advice when looking for a photographer is to make sure you find someone who represents your style and aesthetic and to do your research on their professionalism, personality, and organization. On your wedding day, the time goes quickly and every minute truly matters. Find someone whom you can trust to not miss any of it and who will help keep you on track, while also calming nerves, grounding you, and reminding you what truly matters.

Chapter 11

Reimagine Planning

As the industry continues to grow every year, so does the need for qualified, professional vendors, especially wedding planners. Things are shifting from small weddings held in church banquet halls to large scale, elaborate events. And although I think my mom is *still* a little stunned I didn't get married in a church, I could not be more excited about all the changes on the wedding planning scene.

Laurie Hartwell, CEO and founder of The Bridal Society, saw the need to train and mentor up-and-coming wedding planners and to help train them to be industry professionals and skilled leaders. With over twenty years of experience, she has taught hundreds of intensive training courses all over the United States, teaching members the ins and outs of the industry and giving them opportunities to practice what they have learned.

Laurie Hartwell is an inspiration to many in the wedding industry, including me, and recently was awarded the title "Most Helpful Mentor" from WeddingWire. Through her inspiration to so many and significant influence on the industry, Laurie has truly helped the industry reimagine wedding planners' influence on the wedding day and industry at large.

* * *

When I first heard of The Bridal Society, it was from my first wedding planning "boss" and mentor who eagerly encouraged me to participate and get plugged into the community. After researching and learning about how professional and uplifting this community was, I was on a plane and heading to South Florida (so my educational trip could turn into a mini vacay). Flying solo, arriving in this beautiful conference space, and doing it all by myself at barely twenty years old I remember not feeling scared but rather *empowered*. I was putting my money where my mouth was. I was taking steps to actually make my dreams a reality. And I was so excited!

Through this training, my ideas and thoughts were validated. Before this, I saw changes and saw my brides wanted to do things differently. But arriving in this space validated that even more.

In the certification course, as well as in our later conversations, Laurie discussed on how this industry is changing and how wedding planning is changing too. Laurie, The Bridal Society, and so many other certified wedding planners are truly reimagining wedding planning.

* * *

Let's think back to the 1980s and 1990s of wedding planning. Were you even alive? I wasn't. In those days, technology and media were non-existent. Cell phones weren't a thing, and neither was posting on social media. In-person meetings and phone calls were all that you really had.

Fast forward to today and we are abounding with wedding planning tools, certified professionals, and endless online resources. The advancements of technology and social media have enhanced every business sector, but especially in small business and creative industries. We can find clients, build relationships, and connect with vendors.

I cannot imagine running my business without the use of technology. Every day I am emailing clients, updating our Google Drive documents, posting on Instagram, updating my website, writing a blog post, researching SEO advancements...the list goes on and on.

Not only has the industry shifted in the way technology is used, but also the industry has totally shifted in how Generation Z and millennial couples are shopping for wedding professionals and communicating with them. As a Gen Z bride, AND a Gen Z vendor, I have been on both sides of this. When looking to hire someone, I begin by stalking their social media (as I'm sure that brides have stalked mine.)

So as a bride, let me get in your mind for a second. You start by thinking *"I need to hire this vendor"* and maybe do some simple googling or ask your friends on social media. Next, you probably pull up their Facebook or Instagram sites, look at their posts, images, and past reviews. Then, if you like what you see, you will go to their website and do a little more investigating. If this checks out, a Facebook message, an Instagram DM, a contact form, or an email is sent. Then you sit back and wait for an immediate reply. Am I right?

This is just one small example of how planning your wedding and finding vendors through technology is drastically changing the planning process. In years prior, wedding professionals didn't have to worry if their Instagram feed was cohesive or if they were replying to messages fast enough.

* * *

Wedding planning today is also about customizing. It's about ordering specialized and beautiful products and planning each and every wedding differently from the one before it. Laurie reflects on this saying, "We aren't just doing the same thing over and over again, just because that's what the last wedding did." As a wedding planner myself, I agree that this makes it more fun and interesting when clients do different things and want to make their wedding about their unique love story. Today's couples are shying away from the traditional, are more relaxed, and just want to have fun.

Laurie notes another planning cliché that is changing is that fact that it's "the bride's day." It is finally becoming understood and accepted that is not about making all of the events and every detail accommodate one person (traditionally the bride) but instead a day to celebrate the love of two people and the start of their new lives together. In traditional marriages, we see the groom take a backseat, but in recent years, grooms are getting more of the spotlight. Trends such as "groom's cakes" are skyrocketing and elaborate "groom's suites" in the venues are now a must when booking.

Also, I believe that the legalization of gay marriage in 2015 also contributed to this shift. Instead of focusing on "the bride," the day became centered around the "couple." The celebration focused on the couple's unique story and they made most of the decisions together, giving them permission to rewrite traditions and customize their day. Laurie adds saying, "It's about the *couple* that is getting married. And it really does need to be customized to who they are. What are their hobbies? What do they like to do? What would represent them the best?" These are the questions that we should be asking of the couple as a whole, not just focusing on the bride and what she wants.

Speaking of what the couple wants, let's talk about how this relates to planning trends. Wedding planners, photographers, and everyone in between loves to talk about trends. What is trending in colors, decor, fashion, food...the list goes on. Although I love giving brides (and anyone who will listen) my two cents worth on what trends I am personally loving, Laurie provided a unique perspective about how she approaches trends. Instead of giving *her* opinion about trends, colors, or ideas that her clients have selected, Laurie says she encourages the couple to voice their thoughts and opinions. It is not her job to change their ideas but to take their ideas and make them beautiful and current. What the couple selects should be entirely up to them; this isn't our chance to style our dream wedding to build our portfolio. It's our responsibility to honor our couple and make their dreams a reality. Let's change planning in this way– don't plan your wedding to the industry standard. Plan it, style it, and pick details that are what you as a couple love.

And a side note to wedding planners or industry vendors...

Part of being successful in this industry is not only keeping up with the trends, but being willing to accept new ideas and create trends of your own. As wedding professionals, it is not our job to state our personal opinion about colors, decor, or anything else that the couple decides on, even if we have seen it a million times before. Instead, we need to be accepting of their choices, offer our professional opinion when they want it, and give creative suggestions and embrace new trends when we see them coming.

It used to be the "trendy" thing to have head tables covered in tulle in a banquet hall, or tablecloth overlays that only go halfway down the table. Those trends were very "in" at the time. Looking back on the current era of the industry, the "in" thing will be getting married in barns and having mix-matched bridesmaids dresses.

Although I still love serving my clients by giving them up-to-date information on what is trending and researching popular, new ideas, I think it is also important to remember that at the end of the day, it is most important that your client feels heard and that his or her ideas are being represented in the wedding. As professional wedding planners, it is our job to point out ideas that will inhibit the flow of the event, such as not having enough seating for guests or not having a planned time for dinner. However, ensuring clients listen and implement trend ideas is not our job. Sure, if they ask for recommendations, trend ideas, color schemes, or anything, I want to give them my professional opinion. But at the end of the day, it is my job to execute a flawless wedding that perfectly reflects the couple, which is going to get more and more unique as Generation Z steps into the spotlight.

Planning for Generation Z
Generation Z is pushing boundaries and experimenting with fun ideas, even more so than millennials. As I am working with brides from my generation, I see them

approach planning very differently. As mentioned above, relying on technology for all aspects of communication and organization is key for Gen Z. They also are willing to spend a bit more on customization or products that highlight their values.

Laurie comments on another way Gen Z will reimagine and approach planning differently from what we see today. Laurie says, "I think it's going to be more celebrations of the time they have been together, rather than just marriage.". Based on statistics, the average age for marriage in America is twenty-seven years old, but this could be pushed back later for Generation Z couples. Millennials have shaken the industry norm, getting married in barns, having different food, and pursuing destination weddings. However, Gen Z is going to handle things completely differently and it's going to be very interesting. Laurie commented, "Generation Z is going to take a completely different route. We're going to see smaller events that are more intimate. I think that we are going to see people waiting longer to get married. If they don't want to get married, I see them throwing huge elaborate parties to celebrate huge anniversaries, instead."

And throughout the planning, hopefully they will continue to look to trusted wedding planners to help execute their visions. Planners are now bringing more to the table than ever before, especially if they are certified. They have vendor connections, a strong and creative network, and have seen many creative ideas. They can be the missing piece to bringing together your vision and executing your dream day.

Being a wedding planner myself, I loved specifically talking to Laurie about ways wedding planners can do a better job serving their clients. And at the end of the day, we as wedding planners truly want to serve our clients by helping them. We want to inspire you to reimagine the importance of wedding planners and the role we play in making your wedding the wedding of your dreams. I believe that there are some misconceptions around wedding professionals, especially wedding planners, by those inside and outside of the industry. We don't just look up ideas on Pinterest and boss people around. I want to challenge those outside of the industry, especially my brides reading this, to see the true value of wedding planners and to understand that true skill and training goes into this. Pinterest, a magazine, or an online website cannot offer the same amount of guidance. Unfortunately, overall, the misconception is that wedding planners don't really do much more than an average person. But I hope you learn that we truly guide, coach, lead, and serve the bride, groom, and their families.

Laurie best sums it up, saying, "I feel like being a wedding planner is more than just organizing the details. And it's more than just making things beautiful. It's about making sure that the experience of planning such a beautiful and memorable event is looked upon in a positive way in the years after."

Chapter 12

Reimagine Dresses

The wedding dress–*the* dress that brides dream about, sometimes since they were little girls. The stigma around finding the perfect dress makes most brides feel a lot of pressure and so many brides I've talked to end up changing their minds when picking out a wedding dress. I am almost embarrassed to admit that I was one of them.

My mom and I blocked off a weekend dedicated to wedding dress shopping so the pressure to find "the one" over that weekend was already weighing me down. Secondly, we made reservations at a high-demand bridal boutique that was jam packed with people and had one of my college friends as our sales associate, putting even more pressure on me to pick something. We were also there for over *six hours*, trying on every dress that was in my size and striking out with nearly all of them. Finally, one of the final dresses I tried on looked the best out of any other I had tried during this appointment and in our stress, exhaustion, and pressure, my mom and I decided that this was "the best option." I sincerely liked the dress, but I knew in the back of my mind I didn't *love it*. I was looking to my mom and friends for support, but they weren't giving me the reaction I was hoping for either. I felt defeated.

Don't worry—I ended up finding the dress of my dreams, thanks to one of my bridesmaids. She was thrift shopping at our local Goodwill, and she saw...the dress. It was in its original garment bag, in new condition besides a little dirt on the hem, was my exact size, and was a high-end wedding boutique brand with the original value close to $5,000. I couldn't believe it. And the kind cashier at Goodwill only charged me $20 for it and gave me a recommendation of where to get it dry cleaned for less than $50. It was definitely meant to be.

One of my best friends is also getting married and she texted her girlfriends in our group chat, "I found my dress!!!" It was beautiful and we all loved it. And then she texted me the next day, saying she had cried all night about her decision, changed her mind, went back to the salon, and found *another* dress. I encouraged her she wasn't alone.

But through my experience, my friend's experience, and so many other brides whom I have worked with or seen posting for help in forums, this is *common*! Doubting your dress, changing your mind, and finding something else happens regularly. There is so much uncertainty, doubt, stress, and pressure that surrounds this decision, and it's a very emotional time for everyone involved.

And the huge price tag associated with it doesn't help the pressure and emotions. The average wedding dress costs $1,050 according to WeddingWire, and in 2018 the price escalated to $1,700[95]. And this is without factoring in costs of alterations, accessories, and dry cleaning! The average cost of alterations range from $200-$400 and undergarments and accessories such as jewelry and shoes can get really expensive as well![96]

I find myself falling into this mindset, and therefore, I'm sure other Gen Zs do: *why are we spending so much money on something we will only wear once?* And if I'm spending so much money on such an important item, I want it to be *unique* and *different*.

In my research I have found some amazing, forward-thinking companies who are doing an extraordi-

---

95   "Wedding Dress Cost Guide| Weddingwire". 2019. *Weddingwire.*
96   Ibid

nary job helping brides navigate this stressful decision, while giving them access to unique options and the online resources that Generation Z expects. These are the companies that are revolutionizing the wedding dress shopping experience and I think Generation Z will especially be drawn to this new way of doing things.

Samantha Sleeper, called a "wedding dress whisperer" by *Forbes*, is a Parsons School of Design graduate, sewing and creating beautiful wedding dresses in New York City.[97] Sleeper sources her supplies for her dresses locally, supporting niche small businesses, and practicing sustainability and ethical sourcing[98]; all so important to Gen Z. Sleeper says, "My approach is to always understand my client, her love story, and her perception of marriage,"[99] and uses this mindset to create beautiful gowns. According to their website, Samantha Sleeper and her team custom make dresses in 4-6 months based on each client's specific measurements. This not only saves money on the alteration process (since no alterations are needed) but is more inclusive of brides who are not the standard sample size.[100]

---

97   Sweeney, Deborah. 2019. "7 Innovative Entrepreneurs Revolutionizing The Wedding Industry". Forbes.Com.

98   Ibid

99   Ibid

100 Ibid

Millennials have started the customization trend and have opened up the online world, with thirty-five percent shopping for their wedding dress online[101]. However, being the digital natives that they are, Gen Z is going to continue this trend of online research and shopping. Combined with their strong desire for customization, ideas such as this are going to be huge. According to the website, Samantha Sleeper says, "Our gowns are all custom made to an individual's measurements and no alternations are needed. For clients, we have added secret pockets, hand painted, made a breast-feeding accessible dress, and created a ballgown that transforms into a jumpsuit."[102] The investment in a Samantha Sleeper custom-designed dress begins at $3,000, which although higher than the industry average, is not much more expensive than most boutique bridal brands. Her dresses are stunning, truly one-of-a-kind, and most of it can be done via online research and only a trip or two to the NYC location, creating your perfect dream dress.

Another option that I am familiar with is a sustainable bridal boutique in my college town. This store is called Church Street Bridal and receives sample dresses from

101   Rosen, Ellen. 2019. "Online Retailers Aim To Shake Up The Wedding Market". *Nytimes.Com.*

102   Sweeney, Deborah. 2019. "7 Innovative Entrepreneurs Revolutionizing The Wedding Industry". *Forbes.Com*

high-end bridal boutiques across the east coast such as Kleinfeld Bridal. These dresses are clean and in pristine condition, never worn by an actual bride down the aisle, but only as sample dresses to try on in the store. They have price tags of thousands of dollars and are discounted to $100-$500 depending on the brand and detailing of the dress. These dresses are stunning and really affordable and are definitely worth the trip, if you fall into the average sample size of 4-12, with several outliers in other sizes as well.

A final option that I discovered in my research is called Anomalie, another custom-design wedding dress experience. In this experience, brides never have to leave the comfort of their home and the entire process is done online. Anomalie says they "...bring more transparency, customization, and value to wedding dress shopping by partnering with the world's top dress designer workshops and selling directly to brides online."[103] This cuts the price drastically because the "middleman" of shop retailers are cut out of the equation while still bringing the bride the customization and quality craftsmanship she values.

---

103 "Anomalie | How To Design A Wedding Dress Online". 2019. *Anomalie*.

Anomalie's process takes around 12 months from the initial consultation to the dress arriving on your doorstep. The process starts with a phone call and a design consultation, reviewing the bride's inspiration photos, discussing her vision, and figuring out the style of her dream dress.[104] After this, the bride and designer collaborate. The designer will send sketches and fabric swatches and beading samples, ensuring everything is the quality and style you will love. After your measurements are finalized, it takes four months for the creation of the dress, and a few weeks more for the dress of your dreams to arrive at your front door. Dresses from Anomalie begin at $1,000 and the process is entirely through phone calls and online resources.[105] These dresses also look so stunning, and the sketches and dresses look identical!

I was so inspired through my research of these companies and I know I would have pursued one of these non-conventional options, if I was not so lucky to find the dress of my dreams at a thrift store. I hope that these options will inspire you and give you hope that you aren't stuck in the option of going to a local bridal boutique and spending thousands of dollars on a dress that isn't customized to you. The sustainability, tech

---

104   Ibid

105   Rosen, Ellen. 2019. "Online Retailers Aim To Shake Up The Wedding Market". *Nytimes.Com.*

aspects, customization, and unique experience check all the boxes Gen Z seeks.

Chapter 13

Reimagine Flowers

Baby's breath. Giant ribbons. Ordering from the same florist on downtown main street that probably made your prom corsage (and your mom's, too). That's just what you did back in the '80s and even in the years beyond. Years ago, flowers were traditional. They were made with the flowers that were in season and the hotel ballroom would display matching centerpieces as the brides and bridesmaids would hold their matching bouquets. If you still can't imagine this, ask your mom to show you her wedding photos and you might get the idea.

Flowers have shifted dramatically since then and brides are going one of two routes: they are either doing DIY or letting a luxury florist take care of things. I was able to dive into both these options, and it is interesting to see how flowers are becoming such a key part of the wedding day, regardless of the route the couple takes.

I first had the opportunity to interview luxury florist, Mary Ellen from Steelcut Flower Co. She is one of my favorite florists I've encountered because of her organic, ethereal style and her entrepreneurial spirit. Arguably, the florist is the vendor who brings life to and transforms the wedding space through the flowers she uses. The venue is her canvas and she uses her flowers to paint a story. Flowers are very powerful in setting the tone for weddings and decorating the space.

Raised on a flower farm, Mary Ellen always loved flowers, but as she was growing up, she expresses that flowers were not really "accepted" as beautiful decor or something to buy "just because." When at farmers' markets, people glanced at the flowers, wondering what they were supposed to "do with them" and she felt uninspired by the traditional stigma that surrounded the industry. Plain, formal, and matching bouquets were all that Mary Ellen saw and she wanted to change that.

Florists are transforming their craft and taking more creative freedoms due to the open-mindedness of millennials (their current clients), and this is changing how they are seen by the industry. They are creating elaborate displays for ceremony sites and backdrops that are "Instagram worthy," which is definitely important to younger millennials and even more important to Gen Z.

* * *

The shift of flowers being seen and accepted as an art form has truly evolved in recent years. Even as recently as a decade ago, traditional, formal, uniform flowers were the normal wedding flowers. As Mary Ellen and I chatted, we agreed that the large bulk of this shift can be attributed to social media. In years past, inspiration and resources had to be pulled from local vendors or magazines, whereas today, Instagram and Pinterest have opened a world of opportunity for vendors and brides alike. Weddings have shifted and grown because of the wealth of resources available to us through a quick web search or following a hashtag. We can connect with people, collaborate, and be inspired by styles without leaving the comfort of our homes. Although social media gets a bad reputation, it is truly inspiring and brings creatives together from across the world and has given creators the opportunity for their work to finally be seen and accepted as an art form of self-expression. On the flip side, we also discussed how it can set up unrealistic expectations, which can be detrimental to the industry. Although these resources help give vendors more ideas and push them outside their comfort zones, it sets the expectations high and can harm our careers when clients have unrealistic exceptions.

Not only can social media provide us with great inspiration, but also it is one of the most powerful marketing tools for small businesses and wedding entrepreneurs, especially if clients are posting your work and marketing your brand. Florists have been and need to continue setting themselves up for success for referrals and posts. The easiest way to do this for vendors, and florists specifically, is to give Generation Z something incredible to post about and share with their friends. Obviously, this should not be the entire reason to create, but when creators are making beautiful things, why not post about it and use social media in your favor?

Generation Z especially loves being hands-on while creating, thus making the "do-it-yourself" approach to flowers so popular. This can be done in a variety of ways and on large and small scales. Some choose to go to craft stores such as Michael's or Hobby Lobby and making customized bouquets out of faux flowers. Before you discredit this idea and think it's tacky, these stores have really stepped up their game with their faux flower selection and have beautiful options that look very real.

There are pros to this route, such as not worrying about your flowers wilting during the event or being able to re-purpose the flowers after the wedding. Some also argue that this is more "sustainable" and resourceful since the flowers can be up-cycled and re-purposed, while others say that using real flowers are better for the environment. Locally-sourced flowers from local flower farms and designed by local vendors, or the bride herself, are another great option and a way to support small businesses, be eco-friendly, and have a customized look.

In my research, I came across Flower Moxie, which is an alternative flower shop that empowers brides to make beautiful DIY arrangements with real flowers. Here's a little step-by-step about the vision of Flower Moxie and how it all works:[106]

1. You pick out your flower arrangements online and browse numerous color schemes, styles, and types of flowers.
2. After you decide on the colors and styles you want, browse Flower Moxie's online resources. They have dozens of video tutorials, pre-made collections, printable floral "recipes" and experienced floral designers to help you through the process.
3. After you select your color scheme, and package size, Flower Moxie ships these fresh flowers directly

---

106 "Flower Moxie - How Does It All Work". 2019. *Flower Moxie.*

to your door. You place your order three to four months before your big day and have your flowers delivered about three days before your event and construct your bouquet.

4. Have a blast DIYing your beautiful arrangements with the people you love. As you're prepping for the wedding weekend, grab your bridesmaids, moms, and friends for a girls' night and make memories making beautiful bouquets over a wine and cheese board (my suggestion, but I'm sure Flower Moxie would agree this is a fun idea, too)

Pros of DIYing with Flower Moxie is that they can help you save money, their site is easy to figure out, and your flowers are totally customizable, not to mention fun. Flower Moxie's website is super organized and walks you through the process of how to go about constructing the bouquets of your dreams. With a printable checklist, helpful videos, and detailed photos, anyone could turn into a rockstar florist for a day and make their own gorgeous bouquet.

Flower Moxie is a revolutionary idea that I am certain will catch on, especially with Generation Z. As research by ThinkSplendid previously suggested, Gen Z takes an entirely new approach to DIY, looking at it as part of their everyday life and who they are as a person[107]. For this reason, along with the variety of customization, options, ability to engage through technology, as well as the experience of creating with your closest friends and family, I think the concept of Flower Moxie will pick up with millennials but grow exponentially as Gen Z steps into the spotlight. Creating small businesses, such as Flower Moxie, that are an online retailer with a strong brand that is giving creativity and customization back to the bride are checking nearly every box that Generation Z looks for when selecting a product or service.

---

107   Stevens, Liene. 2019. "2019 State Of The Wedding Industry · Think Splendid®". *Think Splendid®*.

Chapter 14

Reimagine Rings

The ring—it is usually the highlight of the ceremony. The tangible symbol of commitment that the couple shares together, and wears for the rest of their lives to symbolize their never-ending love. Each couple's story is different, just like their engagement ring. Recently, engagement rings have taken a shift from traditional jewelry store diamonds to ethically sourced rings, vintage heirlooms, memorable stones, and more.

But why? Let's learn a little bit about the history of the diamond industry first.

An article from *The Atlantic* highlights the start of the diamond industry and history of engagement rings. Although diamonds were slowly becoming more popular, everything changed when diamonds were discovered in South Africa. In 1880, Cecil Rhodes, with other investors, founded the De Beers Mining Company and within decades, they controlled ninety percent of the world's diamond production. Unfortunately, greed and mass harvesting became the number one priority, and De Beers turned diamond engagement rings into nothing more than an ad campaign.[108]

Starting in the 1940s, De Beers launched its now classic slogan, "A Diamond is Forever," according to the American Gemstone Society[109]. This not only implied the durability of a diamond, but also alluded to the American mindset, especially in that era, that marriage is forever.[110] A diamond became the symbol of the depth of a man's commitment to the woman he loves and became the symbol of love all over the world. Then, the opening of the De Beers mines in Africa made diamonds more accessible to everyone, with mining occurring very frequently.[111]

The engagement ring is usually long planned for and anticipated, kicking off the couple's journey toward a lifetime of love and happiness. However, recent contro-

108 Friedman, Uri. 2019. "How An Ad Campaign Invented The Diamond Engagement Ring". *The Atlantic.*

109 "The History Of Diamond Engagement Rings - American Gem Society". 2019. *Americangemsociety.Org.*

110 Ibid

111 Friedman, Uri. 2019. "How An Ad Campaign Invented The Diamond Engagement Ring". *The Atlantic.*

versy surrounds the diamond industry and consumers, especially Generation Z, are outraged and want to make a difference. If you are not aware, many diamonds are harvested through unethical treatment and exploitation of individuals, usually in Africa[112]. According to research presented by Groundswell, a leader in economic empowerment, a "conflict diamond" is any diamond mined in a war zone and sold to finance armed confrontation.[113] The purchase of conflict diamonds has prolonged bloody battles in the Democratic Republic of the Congo, Angola, Côte d'Ivoire, and Sierra Leone, among other countries.[114] And the worst part is that Western society didn't even know they were financing and prolonging such horrible things. Their blinders were on as they shopped for the brightest and best diamond they could find, without looking beyond the jewelry store.

But Generation Z is different. This generation examines the sourcing of things, looks beyond the issue at hand and wants to address the root of the problem[115]. As countless stories of exploitation and war continue to come out and be linked to the diamond industry,

---

112   "Conflict Diamond Mining". 2019. *Brilliant Earth.*
113   "Blood & Conflict Diamonds". 2019. *Encyclopedia Britannica*
114   Ibid
115   Seemiller, Corey. Ted Talk. 2019. Generation Z: Making A Difference Their Way. Video.

many consumers, especially in the newest generation, are looking to alternative sources and is turning to lab creating diamonds or alternative gemstones.

"Couple" is a luxury diamond brand that specializes in ethically grown, lab sourced diamonds and could be the solution many consumers seek[116]. Couple says that their lab-grown diamonds are atomically and chemically identical to mined diamonds, but they are twenty-five to thirty percent larger on a price basis and meet the highest of standards.[117] Not only is the luxury brand and larger diamond appealing to most consumers, but millennials and Gen Z are very tuned in to sustainability, and ethically sourced goods are important to them. These rings are stunning, customizable (checking another box for Gen Z) and more affordable than a diamond from a leading jewelry store.

Another leader in engagement rings, Brilliant Earth, is also concerned with creating beautiful diamonds with priority on ethically sourced, transparent, and conflict-free jewelry. Brilliant Earth also educates consumers about unethical diamond trade. They say, "the world's diamond mines produce not only diamonds – but also civil wars, violence, worker exploitation,

116   "Our Story | Couple". 2019. *Couple*
117   Ibid

environmental degradation, and unspeakable human suffering."[118] Thankfully, consumers are becoming more aware and shifting away from traditionally sourced diamonds. Ajay Anand, founder of another diamond company Rare Carat, reflects on this industry change, saying, "Consumers are just more empowered than previous generations, and it has tipped the balance in an industry that has historically favored the jeweler, who is omniscient."[119]

Again, millennials led the charge in sustainability from their coffee to their clothing, and Gen-Zers are following behind, demanding transparency and high ethical standards from every industry, including sectors within the wedding industry. Also, in the combined pursuit of ethically sourced jewelry and being unique and authentic, couples are opting for custom designed engagement rings from family heirlooms or non-conventional gemstones. Traditional, established jewelers in brick and mortar stores are becoming overshadowed by online retailers who promise complete satisfaction at better prices and better stewardship.

---

118   "Conflict Diamond Mining". 2019. *Brilliant Earth.*
119   Chaudhuri, Saikat. 2019. "The Company Bringing Clarity To Online Diamond Shopping". *Mack Institute For Innovation Management*

Current brides and grooms who hold tight to traditional mindsets, might not be completely willing to accept this shift. However, since Gen Z was raised on technology and over-stimulation, they are used to the constant waves of new information. With this, they roll with the punches and adapt easily to new ideas. The combination of this unique trend with an ethical issue is the perfect combination for this innovative generation to jump on this industry change.

* * *

Another jewelry shift that is already inspiring Gen Z couples is replacing traditional diamonds with unique gemstones. For several reasons such as trying to save money, being unconventional, or picking a stone that has a certain meaning, Gen-Zers are making the switch to stones such as sapphire, aquamarines, rubies, and more. One of my friends just got engaged and her ring is gorgeous and very unique. It is a light blue gemstone that her father brought back from a tour in Afghanistan. He presented the idea to her fiancé and gave it to him when they talked about their engagement. They custom designed it into a beautiful square cut engagement ring, and not only was my friend surprised by the engagement but also was very touched by the sentimental aspect that it represented.

Another couple I know custom designed a ring with a diamond, emerald, and sapphire in it. The diamond is in the middle, representing their engagement, the emeralds circle the diamond, representing the month they started dating (May) and the Sapphires circle the emeralds, representing the month they met (September). This ring is not only stunning but also has such as unique and meaningful story. My cousin recently got engaged, and her fiancé has family and heritage in Guatemala. Their engagement occurred at their favorite place in Guatemala and her engagement ring was made from jade, which represents his heritage and country.

Generation Z is changing the market for rings that tell their unique love story, and now are able to access them virtually anywhere, as companies are shifting to a one hundred percent online presence. *Vogue* reflects on this transformation, saying, "Because of rapid technological advancements in lab-grown synthetic diamonds and the fact that—thanks to the internet and Instagram—buyers are armed with more information and options than ever before, the engagement ring shopping experience is changing."[120] These companies are rising to the new market with ethical options and customization, which are all key to their up and coming target market.

---

120 Macon, Alexandra. 2019. "7 Ways Engagement Ring-Buying Is Changing". *Vogue*.

So the next time one of your Gen Z friends or clients gets engaged, ask them the story behind their engagement ring. I bet it will check one of these boxes.

Chapter 15

Reimagine Venues

My grandmother and I have a very close relationship and she played a key role in my wedding planning process. Weeks after I got engaged, I excitedly showed her my wedding venue, which was a beautifully renovated manor home tucked in the Blue Ridge Mountains of Central Virginia. She was excited for me while browsing the photos, but quickly asked, "Why aren't you getting married in a church?" I didn't know what to say. I honestly had never considered it because that wasn't what my generation did and that wasn't what appealed to me. I never realized my venue choice would be so polarizing to older generations. I had accepted this transformation without even realizing it.

Wedding venues are transforming from basic churches and traditional ballrooms to unique spaces that tell the couple's story. Gen Z couples choose things that have meaning to them, and the venue is no different. Instead of choosing their family church (which they may not have stepped foot in for years) or a banquet hall at the local hotel, they are thinking outside the box as much as possible.

One of my favorite weddings I've ever attended was at a charming waterfront park in the Charleston, South Carolina area. This park was off the beaten path, near a beautiful canal and the historic oak trees made a beautiful ceremony background. Included was a historic house that had been transformed into a reception location for around one hundred people. A string-light covered open patio was the dance floor and it was so intimate and romantic. This was also the location of the couple's first date, and when I learned that, my heart just about burst. Knowing how the venue tied into their love story made the day even more special.

The venue, in case you are unfamiliar with this "wedding term," basically means the location where the wedding reception, cocktail hour, and/or ceremony occurs. It is the background of the day. The canvas on which the long-anticipated moments of love and forever unfold. Arguably, one of the most important elements of the entire wedding–the place it all begins.

But unfortunately, it also seems to be the costliest and the most ambiguous. Browsing online for venues is a draining process and it is hard to determine what is truly included, what the layout of the venue is, and to envision the most important day of your life happening there; let alone, trying to determine if the ceremony AND reception are happening there. And what about cocktail hour? And the rehearsal? The questions and options keep bombarding you and the decision seems overwhelming.

Although the need for unique wedding venues is rising, couples seem to be having a harder time connecting and finding the right location. One reason is that venues get booked years in advance. One of my best friends who isn't even engaged yet has her wedding venue booked. Don't worry, she does have a boyfriend and knows the proposal is coming soon so she's not completely crazy... she just knows the place she wants and that her month is a super popular time, so she wanted to act fast!

Other reasons finding the perfect place is difficult is due to the lack of amenities that are included. A place might be beautiful and unique, but if it lacks essential items such as tables and chairs, which are obviously important, that is a deterrent to the couple. And although they aren't expensive to rent, the time and added stress doesn't make it worth it. Finally, the biggest reason finding the perfect venue is difficult is the non-transparency in pricing, which adds extra stress on the bride and groom. Finances are always a touchy subject and it's even more emotional in the wedding industry.

I understand this process and the feelings all too well because it happened to me not too long ago. Getting engaged in the same college town where I started my wedding career was such a special experience. My fiancé and I knew we wanted to involve some of our favorite vendors and small-town companies into our special day, and I immediately started contacting my list of venues. We browsed the online resources, looked at images, and looked at their websites. And before long, we noticed something that was consistent on nearly every website regardless of the location or style of the venue: there were no prices.

I would email companies, and some would send me documents and information. Some were helpful, some were not. Spreadsheets, charts, and grids with different options, and different prices all depending on the season, the year, if you were having your ceremony, cocktail hour, and reception there. Comparing the places was nearly impossible and sorting through the costs and fees was overwhelming. I wanted the place to be perfect, but I also wanted it to be unique and affordable. These things didn't seem to align.

Through this process, I tried to refer to documents I received from the wedding company I worked with several years before who not only offered planning services, but also had multiple venues under their control. I was shocked to realize that even in my resources from them, I couldn't find a thing regarding pricing. I understand that vendors want to keep their prices hidden from their competitors, but there needs to be a middle ground.

I did some industry research to see if anyone else was frustrated like I was or if this was just a trend in my area. Apparently, it impacts many couples and the available resources aren't quite getting the job done.

Wedding planning duo Christy Matthews and Michelle Martinez sat down with venue guru Veronica Armstrong and delved into this issue on their podcast, *The Big Wedding Planning Podcast*. I was so grateful to hear their input on this and it made me feel not so alone on this topic. They agree that the industry is changing and transforming and discuss how despite some mega changes, the industry seems to be "stuck."[121] Armstrong says, "We as wedding professionals want to change the

---

121 Matthews, Christy, and Michelle Martinez. 2019. "#126 Unique Venues, Unique Perspective: Mayflower Venue's Veronica Armstrong". Podcast. *The Big Wedding Planning Podcast.*

industry, but what I would beg the wedding industry to do is to just take a hard look at how they're operating."[122]

Although venues may be operating in a trendy manor and running successful day-to-day operations, the price-point seems to be a sticky subject that is keeping the industry from reaching its full potential. Also, the industry is operating so robotically at times that the personal aspect of each wedding is getting lost in the mix. It's not that the budget is always an issue and that clients are unwilling or unable to pay the prices; it's the fact that numbers seem hidden or that prices are manipulated, and fees are added. As the conversation continues, Armstrong added, "I think that the wedding industry, if they don't want to change, they're going to be forced to change because customers are demanding transparency like every other industry in the world."[123] When you look at any other industry, such as fashion or consumer services, products have price tags and services have set prices. It doesn't depend on the client or the time of the year. It is fairer and more transparent.

A solution they discovered is called "Mayflower Venues," which is a brand new concept in the northeastern United States. They call themselves the "Airbnb

---

122 Ibid
123 Ibid

of Wedding Venues," and allow different locations that could "work" as a wedding venue advertise their location on their website.[124] Veronica Armstrong, their representative, explains a little more about how their service works, saying, "What we do is we allow couples to discover these rare, non-traditional wedding venues, things like farms, barns, estates, cranberry bogs, oyster farms...you can discover all of that on our site. And from there, we allow you to customize your wedding."[125] The possibilities are endless and are truly a destination and will make the wedding unique. However, not only are these venues offering unique locations, they are one hundred percent transparent with their services, costs, and what is included. Mayflower Venues requires their venues to list everything from the size of spaces, how many chairs, tables, decorations, etc. are included, and the exact price—upfront and available from the very beginning.[126]

This is going to be big. And just as Airbnb turned the hotel industry around and rocked its foundation, it's just a matter of time before this does the same. Consumers want transparency and consistency. And especially in this industry, they want to feel unique, special, and like

124 Ibid
125 Ibid
126 "How It Works". 2019. *Mayflower Venues*

their wedding day is truly the most memorable day of their lives.

Generation Z also values technology, so the fact that this venue experience is becoming digital is also key. Being able to view the space from the convenience of their living room while getting questions answered and booked completely online is going to make this venue experience truly like nothing else. Furthermore, making the venue customizable, including as much as possible, to help serve the bride and groom is appealing. As the industry continues to evolve, individuality is becoming the new norm—each couple wants the venue to tell their story. And in the industry, we need to back them up and give them every means possible to do so.

Letting the venue be the ultimate personal touch seemed to be a concept that the industry was missing for a while. There's only so much a couple can customize about their flowers, decor, and food. Having a unique background that highlights their personal style and one-of-a-kind love story can add the ultimate personal touch.

PART 4

Chapter 16

Industry Reflections & Improvements

In any industry or career, there are some things you love about it and something you would rather change. I'm thankful to admit that overall, I love the community and creativity that the wedding industry has to offer and the role that wedding professionals play in a couple's big day. However, I think it would be wrong for me not to highlight areas I think we all, as wedding professionals, can improve on. I love this quote by T.D. Jakes which says, "If you always do what you've always done, you'll always be where you've always been."[127] Without self-reflection and looking at areas for improvement, we will not grow. We can always do better and there is always room to improve, so we should always seek that. So after talking to some industry leaders, listening to those with more experience, and doing some of my

---

127   Anderson, Amy. 2019. "T.D. Jakes: The Instinct To Succeed". *SUCCESS*

own research, these are some of my reflections about how we as wedding professionals can come together to improve the wedding industry at large.

Communication:
First is the issue of communication. There is definitely miscommunication between the clients, vendors, and guests throughout the wedding planning process. And as is true in all areas of life, lack of communication can lead to major issues down the road. Many wedding vendors do not talk to each other before or even during the wedding day, which can lead to serious problems. When there is no joint communication, and only separate vendors trying to rely on what the couple told them individually, wires can get crossed and there is no plan on the wedding day. This can lead to major issues, especially if some of the vendors are not professional or are inexperienced.

Wedding planning veteran Laurie Hartwell had a great analogy for hiring a wedding vendor or planner who is not trained, or who (worse yet) is a family member or friend. Laurie says, "When you're relying on information from people who have never done this before in their life, that's like saying, "Hi, I need an operation. But I want the doctor who has only been on staff for one day." It doesn't make sense that someone who has no experience in this industry is the one giving all the information." Professional experience and communication is key!

To understand the importance of communication a little better, let's look at how vendors interact on the day of the wedding. Usually, the photographer is with the couple and wedding party as they are getting ready, and other vendors such as the florist, baker, caterer, DJ, and other vendors arrive closer to the event start time. Everyone is going in a million different directions, focusing on their specific task and is not worried about communicating with other vendors. For example, the florist and photographer may not really talk, or even be at the venue at the same time, yet the florist may have key pieces that the photographer needs to capture, or the florist may want to communicate to the photographer to not take "detail shots" of the flowers until she finishes setting up. When vendors are not working near or with each other, they look for a messenger who knows what is going on and who they can trust to ensure the message is received. Which is the wedding planner–*the key communicator.*

So what is the solution to communication issues? First, it's the wedding planner being *extremely* organized and professional, establishing communication expectations with the vendors as soon as the couple books them. It also requires that the other vendors who are booked be professional and strong communicators–answering emails and calls. This also means being clear about the vendors' time of arrival, what they are bringing, setting up, time needed, and more. After the wedding planner has gathered the essential basics, forming authentic connections is so important. These not only help during the stressful times on the wedding day, but helps the vendors trust you and pass that trust on to their client when they are communicating apart from you.

For example, if you as a certified wedding planner *know* that it is going to take 150 guests at least an hour to an hour and a half to eat their meals, yet the catering company is trying to establish a new schedule and claims it could take 30 minutes, the couple is getting mixed messages. However, if relationships have been formed, the wedding planner and caterer could talk about the timeline together first and come to an agreement and then let the wedding planner communicate the final decision with the bride. This will not only establish legitimacy for all vendors when they aren't contradicting each other, but also make the planning process easier when only one person is creating the timeline and communicating with the couple about major decisions. Laurie sums it up best saying, "All [vendors] need to learn each other's language, and have better communication with each other leading up to the wedding day." This will lead to a less stressful and more enjoyable event all the way around.

Transparency:

This is one of my biggest pet peeves, regardless of the situation, and I believe compromises both vendors' and the industry's reputation. Being "transparent" is defined as "having thoughts, feelings, or motives that are easily perceived."[128] Of course, everyone wants to be treated fairly and honestly in any business, feeling they are getting fair value for their money. As discussed in earlier chapters, there is a lack of transparency being recently discussed in venues, with Mayflower Venues providing the solution consumers crave. Unfortunately, the lack of transparency is inching its way into other sectors, especially with regard to hiring vendors and ensuring they are professionals.

Recently, Laurie Hartwell (the CEO and founder of The Bridal Society mentioned previously) and her staff have started a new sector of The Bridal Society through a

---

128 "Definition Of Transparent | Dictionary.Com". 2019. *Www.Dictionary. Com.*

vendor accreditation program. The Bridal Society's mission through all of their courses is "To raise the standards for wedding professionals and for the wedding industry." They do this by "offer[ing] a pathway to accreditation that is affordable and accessible for business owners who wish to distinguish themselves in their field."[129] Besides mentoring and training wedding professionals, TBS wants to "raise awareness among engaged couples about the importance of hiring highly qualified professionals for their wedding needs."[130]

Many relationships in a variety of industries are established through referrals, which can be good or bad. We ask our friends for recommendations on products and services and trust their reviews and opinions. Now in the world of weddings, the same concept originally existed. For example, if you as a caterer worked several times as a well-established and respected venue, they may start recommending you to brides looking for a caterer. This can work in the interest of small businesses, especially if connected to a strong venue because most clients are attracted to and book a venue before they book anything else. When the venue is established and holds themselves to a high standard, they only rec-

129 "The Bridal Society - Who We Are". 2019. *TheBridalSociety.Com.*
130 Ibid

ommend legitimate vendors to their clients; thus making a great network and easy experience for the couple.

This is great if done honestly. However, recommendations are losing their transparency and can be based on friendships, alliances, or vendors paying each other or giving discounts if they are recommended. The industry now has started taking this a step further and has created a "preferred vendors list." Think of this as a "club" that only recommends each other and only works with the people on the list. Some vendors tell you that they won't work with you, the client, unless you sign a contract and only work with their people on their list. Others charge you fees if you want to work with an "outsider." Not only is this manipulative and non-transparent to the couple, it is destructive to others in the industry who are working hard and trying to build connections, but are being killed by the monopoly of the "preferred vendors list."

I know personally when I was searching for vendors, it was extremely difficult for me to sift through lists of companies on websites, examine reviews, and get recommendations from the vendors and my friends. I felt like transparency was missing, and I was selecting people for the most important day of my life based on Facebook reviews or others' recommendations. Laurie addressed how there needs to be more regulations and higher standards in order to combat biased recommendations, letting inexperienced people try to take care of you on the most important day of your life. Thankfully, TBS is raising the bar and setting high industry standards.

Now, in no way am I trying to discourage "newbies." Obviously, everyone starts somewhere and builds their business. And in my opinion, the biased recommendations and exclusive lists are prohibiting new people from getting started and becoming successful. However, many new vendors are afraid to admit that they haven't professionally worked events before, so they create a website or Facebook page and get a few friends to leave reviews and hope that this will be enough to get them booked and out in the community working events. Now, sometimes this works because they can trick people with their experience, but is this really what *you*, a client, want or deserve on the most important day of your life?! Again, there is a lack of transparency AND lack of community. Which we will get to in just a moment...

Community:

If you are unfamiliar with the creative industry, there's a saying that is popular. It's a hashtag, on cute stationary, and is bantered around by small business owners: "Community Over Competition." But what exactly does this mean? Through my research and my own experience, it basically means putting aside our own selfish goals and mindset of competing for success and replacing that with being service-minded and helping others. World-wide wedding photographer Hope Taylor says that from a vendor's perspective, she has seen the industry drastically change from being very "cutthroat" to adopting the concept of "community over competition." Business owners are supporting each other, educating each other and building one another up, instead of holding their knowledge and experience hostage.

I have personally seen this, especially in the photography industry. My personal wedding photographer was actually referred to me by another wedding photographer who had my wedding date booked. Vendors within the same field are working together and collaborating, hosting workshops and planning styled shoots to highlight their talents. Having this mindset of teaming together to support the industry, cheering on our "competitors" and trying to serve clients in the best possible way is key and will be the heartbeat of the wedding industry. If it continues to do it correctly.

Now don't get me wrong; I believe the wedding industry has come leaps and bounds in creating community to serve our clients. And of course, I believe in helping others and forming authentic community. However, I think something is *still* missing and there is room to greatly improve in this mindset.

First, I am discouraged at how many people are approaching this "community over competition" movement with a sense of entitlement. In the name of "community," you feel pressured to give away resources and tricks of the trade that make you "YOU." Knowledge from workshops you paid for and made sacrifices to travel to. Perfect techniques you learned after years of practice. And then just letting someone "pick your brain" after you spend many hours and hard-earned dollars on professional development courses. Let me be the first to say this if you haven't heard it before–you are not required to give your resources, your energy, and your experience to selfish people. Community suggests a relationship that works *both* ways. In the distorted lens and name of "community," do not be a doormat. And don't selfishly ask people for their time and talents just to benefit yourself and your business.

Also, it discourages me to see wedding professionals networking and having strong community with everyone in the wedding industry *except* for those that are in their niche. In non-wedding terms, it looks like a florist being kind, accommodating, referring, and working well with wedding pros like photographers, DJs, wedding planners, venue managers, and everyone else...*except* for other florists in the area. Why? Because they are the *competition*. *Do you get it yet?* This isn't community at all until you are your genuine self and working well with *everyone*. You cannot use this hashtag and boast of this lifestyle and have *selected community*. It doesn't work that way.

That is what frustrates me the most about this industry and the thing I would change. It's the collaborative nature until someone is perceived as a threat. And instead of working hard and collaborating *–and being confident in the unique skills you bring to the table–*it's being threatened and insecure. It's surrounding yourself with a strong set of other vendors, pulling the "preferred vendors list" out as a form of security, and hoping that someone else in your so-called community (read: your competition) will eventually run out of resources and eventually not succeed.

And I am proud to say that although I have encountered fake community in different sectors of my journey, I have never encountered it in the community formed through The Bridal Society and the certification program. This program and these people are different. And I believe that this is in part due to the initiative and courage it takes to pursue your dreams–and we did it together through this program. When you find fellow people taking risks and chasing dreams you want to encourage them too. Laurie empowers people from all over the country to chase their dreams and start their own businesses and promotes the "community over competition" mindset in all she does.

Wedding planners and wedding professionals need to move forward in their confidence and knowledge and take it upon themselves to change the misconceptions the industry and others have about them. We need to advocate for ourselves and our talents as well for our fellow colleagues in this industry. Wedding planners serve their clients more in-depth and personally than many other services will ever be able to provide. This is a career where we make an impact on the most important day of two people's lives, and we shouldn't take that lightly.

Chapter 17

Keys to Success

The phrase "key to success" is often bantered around and determining what voice to listen to and what path to take can be very difficult. As a small business owner trying to find your voice and create your brand, I know it can be especially overwhelming.

If you asked someone what they believe the key to success is, answers would vary, but a few themes would rise to the top. Especially in the wedding industry and creative fields, many people believe that work ethic, strong marketing, or a natural entrepreneurial spirit are the keys. I found myself falling into this mindset as well, believing that my entrepreneurship would keep my business floating. But it didn't always work.

In the midst of purpose-searching and looking for this ambiguous "key to success" I stumbled upon this anonymous quote that changed everything: "I don't know the key to success, but the key to failure is trying to please everybody." That's what I was trying to do–please everyone. And I was failing.

Throughout this journey, I took the opportunity, when talking to successful wedding entrepreneurs, to ask them what they believed they "key to success" was. I also wanted to reflect on my own habits as a Generation Z consumer to see if that mindset would help me find hidden keys for success when planning a wedding for Generation Z. Here are some things I discovered and concepts I wanted to summarize.

1. Strong branding is very important to Generation Z consumers. Whether this is a product or service, I and my peers are drawn to aesthetics and brands who know who they are and for what they stand. Generic brands have a stigma of mistrust and claims of the quality of a product or service isn't going to cut it. Regardless of ads or marketing, researching the personal brand and delving deeper into the product or service is very important to Gen Z, because they can look at any company closer through technology, can research reviews on products and services, and stalk social media they will. So use their research in your favor!

2. Having strong ethical values backing a brand is also important to Generation Z. So many large

companies are starting charitable campaigns, and small businesses are starting to adopt this mindset. Local businesses are locally sourcing products and services, donating to local charities, or are giving away their services to those in need. As wedding professionals, I have peers who will do a photography giveaway for a deserving couple, or caterers who are active in donating leftovers to community shelters. As a Gen Z myself, I know this is an important factor when choosing a product, service, or person. Knowing that people I'm hiring or working with care about others and the community is important as a consumer. Generation Z has access to so many options and can research their options in depth. Therefore, going a step beyond a good product and connecting it to a good cause is key.

3. To Gen Z, being innovative is an expectation, because we as Gen-Zers are very innovative ourselves. This segues into the mindset of creativity and customization that Gen Zs have. We want to be different and put our own spin on things, but don't want it to be *so* different that our peers judge or reject it. As a wedding professional, offering services that can be customized and tailored to each customer will be a key to success. As a wedding planner, this means not offering every client the same three options for decor or as a photographer, taking your couples to

the same locations for engagement shoots. It means thinking outside of the box as your everyday way of thinking.

4. Having stand-out social media is key with Generation Z. With the average Gen Zer having an "eight-second filter" to gauge whether something is worth their attention, small business owners need to make sure their content grabs their attention. Don't be mistaken; this is not the same thing as having a short attention span; we Gen-Zers can focus on things and can have long attention spans. Instead, this "eight-second-filter" is about the average amount of time we will spend determining whether we want to engage with something or someone.

Although this information is key when engaging with the Gen Z audience, I still felt like it didn't hold the "key to success." Next, I interviewed successful wedding professionals, wanting to hear their input.

Hope Taylor, a Gen Z photographer and mentor who's making six figures shared her perspective. Hope says, "I'm a huge believer that photography AND business have to work together in order to be successful, and typically people are more talented in one than the other." I totally agree with this statement, and it relates to all fields. Whether you're a florist, wedding planner, or anything in between, you need to be not only talented at your niche, but also be business-savvy as well. Hope adds, "For me, I LOVE business; however, most creative-minded people struggle with business and marketing. But, if you aren't willing to work hard, hustle and teach yourself about the areas you lack, then success is going to be hard to achieve, if not impossible."

Wow! Go ahead and re-read that last sentence. If you aren't willing to examine your weaknesses, embrace them, and be willing to grow in those areas, it will be extremely hard to be successful! Hope adds, "My biggest piece of advice would be to stay true to who you are, but seek knowledge from industry-leading professionals. Attend workshops and conferences, spend hours on YouTube, invest in one-on-one mentoring: learning from the pros is unlike any other form of learning." When we invest in sharpening ourselves and adapt the mindset that there is always room to learn and grow, we step into success.

I also talked a lot about this with Laurie Hartwell, the founder and CEO of The Bridal Society. Laurie mentioned there are numerous keys to success—not specifically *one way*. I love this—each person's strengths and weaknesses are different, our interests, and our lines of work. However, Laurie mentioned a few that are consistent regardless such as *focus, passion, communication, and positivity.*

- You need to be focused on your goals, whatever they are, in order to accomplish them and make a difference.
- You need to tap into your passion; whatever it is that sets your soul on fire and pursue it. Passion will keep you going when you are discouraged. It will help you remember your why.
- Communication should speak for itself; without strong and professional communication there are mixed messages, everyone will get confused, and businesses and events will crash and burn.
- Finally, positivity keeps you going on the bad days. Surrounding yourself with a team of positive people, inside and outside of your business will keep you focused on the good and looking for the bright side. This line of work is hard. So do not compromise and let negativity in.

But Laurie said believes that there is an ultimate key to success, and that is *integrity.* Integrity means not cutting corners, always doing your best, and being completely authentic. It means going the extra mile when no one is watching, treating others fairly and honorably, and being up front and honest with everyone with whom you come in contact. Laurie sums it up saying, "If you're struggling in the business, it doesn't necessarily mean that you aren't working hard enough, but rather that you aren't focused. Being focused on goals, being confident in yourself, and having a spirit of integrity and authenticity are the many keys to success."

My final thoughts and takeaways from my conversations that I want to pass on to you is this: do not compromise who you are. Find qualified professionals and be a qualified professional. Look not only for professional individuals, but also those who are kind, honest, and take their business seriously. Be someone who communicates openly and offers custom ideas and packages and wants to be there for a couple on the most important day of their life. In this industry, some vendors let their clients blend, taking on too much and not making their clients feel special. As a bride, pick those who will guide you, but let you be yourself. You set yourself up to have the most special day of your life, who are authentic, hard-working, and innovative. And most importantly, look for professionals who want to highlight you and help you and your love story shine.

Chapter 18

Entrepreneurship

Many people think of the word "entrepreneur" as someone who starts their own business in some way, shape or form. However, I want to show you that entrepreneurship goes further than that.

Merriam Webster Dictionary defines *"entrepreneur"* as: "one who organizes, manages, and assumes the risks of a business or enterprise."[131] Risk is key in any entrepreneur's life. Taking a risk in the loan you're taking out, the website you're building, the hours of sacrifice you're putting in that you don't want wasted. It's taking a risk on yourself.

Also according to *Webster's*, the world *entrepreneur* has been in used in the English language to refer to a kind of businessman since at least the middle of the 18th century.[132] During the 19th century, it was also used to

131 "Definition Of ENTREPRENEUR". 2019. *Merriam-Webster.Com.* .
132 Ibid

refer to a person who undertakes any kind of activity, not just a business venture. Furthermore, by the early 20th century *entrepreneur* appears to have taken on the connotation of "go-getter" when applied to an independent business owner,[133] and we commonly hear and use the phrase *entrepreneurial spirit.*

As I scrolled down to the bottom of this dictionary entry, it gave me recent uses of the word in famous articles and research. The top result said: *"There's no better time in the history of the world to be an entrepreneur than right now."*[134]

But what exactly does that mean? All this talk about entrepreneurship and starting your "side-hustle" can be overwhelming, and sounds like a whole other language, especially if you aren't part of the business circle and aren't wired in this way. *Forbes* defines the ambiguous "entrepreneurial spirit" as a **mindset**.[135] *Forbes* continues, "It's an attitude and approach to thinking that actively seeks out change, rather than waiting to adapt to change. This mindset embraces critical questioning,

133   Ibid

134   Westenberg, Jon. 2019. "Why Now Is The Best Time In Human History To Be An Entrepreneur". *Business Insider.*

135   Smith, Jacquelyn. 2019. "How To Keep Your Entrepreneurial Spirit Alive As The Company You Work For Grows". *Forbes.Com*

innovation, service and continuous improvement."[136] I believe that at the core of every entrepreneur are the dream to do things differently and the vision to make a difference. Whether it be the passion to be your own boss, make a splash in your industry niche, or secure your family's future, being an entrepreneur is a passion deep within some people.

My dad has a strong entrepreneurial spirit and he passed that on to me. He's owned his own business for as long as I can remember, and always encouraged me to take the leap of faith, be my own boss, and pursue my dreams. Now I understand this lifestyle and mindset isn't for everyone. Because my mom, on the other hand is very cautious and systematic. Taking risks, especially in the world of business, was not in her nature. And just like my two parents approached the world of entrepreneurship differently, so will the people you come in contact with every day. Some will "click with it" and some won't.

And that's okay.

I don't think it's our responsibility as entrepreneurs to make sure everyone understands what we are doing. It's

---

136 Ibid

not our job and shouldn't be our motive to "change their mind" or "prove them wrong." It's our job to keep working hard every day, crush our goals, and keep moving forward. And by doing this, not only will we succeed, but grow and develop ourselves in the process, thus "proving them wrong."

And believe me, I know this is hard. Especially when you're faced with voices of criticism or are not fully supported by the people around you. But if you let the opinion and voice of one "nay-sayer" (or several) stop you, I don't think you have any business calling yourself an entrepreneur anyway. Let's go back to the definition– it's all about risk and pursuing your dreams and chasing your vision despite obstacles.

* * *

Throughout the process of writing this book, I interviewed and looked to several entrepreneurial individuals in the wedding industry, some whose stories have been mentioned other places in the pages of this book.

Laurie Hartwell, who I refer to throughout the pages of this book, is the founder and CEO of The Bridal Society and leader of the Wedding Planner Certification course. As stated, she also leads the industry in other accreditation programs and mentorship efforts. Laurie has been a professional in this industry since 1993 and shared a little of her backstory with me about how she got started. When she was younger, she would always find herself as the person that people would go to if they were planning a party. "I was kind of born an entrepreneur," Laurie says, "and I just never really wanted to work for anyone else; I needed to be my own boss." Having that entrepreneurial spark in her spirit, Laurie said her first thought was *"How can I turn this into a business?"* When Laurie was wrestling with all of this, it was in the early 1990s, when they didn't really have classes to be a wedding planner. Laurie adds, "There was only one other person in the industry that I knew of in my area that was even doing this. I just knew that this was something I was good at, and something that I thoroughly enjoyed doing. So why not turn something that I love doing into a business?"

I'm sure many wedding entrepreneurs can relate to Laurie's story: her passion ignited her purpose. After falling in love with the industry and deciding to start, Laurie figured out on her own how to market herself and build connections. However, Laurie is the first to humbly admit in her certification courses and in our interview that she made her fair share of mistakes. She shares, "Everybody makes mistakes in the beginning.

That's part of why I teach my certification conferences now, so that I can tell everybody the mistakes I made so that you guys don't do the same." Having that true entrepreneurial spirit is trying again and again, despite your mistakes, because you believe in yourself and in your dream.

Back when Laurie started, cell phones weren't really a big thing and there was no texting. If computers were around, there was one large one in the house and no laptops. There was no Facebook and Instagram did not exist. Younger business owners probably cannot image trying to run a business without these tools, but Laurie still built a successful wedding empire without them. Laurie shares how this stretched her, saying, "I had to really do a lot more in-person meeting and telephone meetings back then." She also had to work to build connections and couldn't rely on technology to make those connections like we do today. She adds, "There was no other place to get out there other than I'm going to have to meet people, I'm going to have to make personal business relationships."

Laurie shares with her students in her courses that she is introverted and starting her business and creating these relationships was very difficult for her at first. She says, "It really took a lot of effort, I had to go to so many networking meetings and just really develop these relationships over time." I would still argue that networking and meeting people face-to-face is the best way to develop and build these relationships, but we are also able to rely on technology and social media to help us build and maintain those relationships. It's more than having an idea and starting a business. It's about getting yourself out there, trying hard, making connections, taking leaps of faith, and believing in yourself.

Because of Laurie's determination to pursue her dreams and believe in her entrepreneurial calling, she is fearlessly leading a national company, The Bridal Society, that is training and raising up wedding industry leaders.

* * *

I wanted the perspective about entrepreneurship from other industry professionals outside of my wedding planning niche, so I also talked about this subject with Mary Ellen, the founder and owner of Steelcut Flower Co. a large East Coast wedding floral company mentioned in the flower chapter Mary Ellen and her team are very passionate and talented, but sometimes feel misunderstood in the wedding industry. Clients and other vendors don't understand all that goes into making a wedding day a reality—the hard work and manual labor of setting up ladders, carrying heavy arrangements and buckets of water (usually in dressy clothes!) as well as the numerous client planning meetings, and the countless hours of behind the scenes work.

The entrepreneurial spirit is what keeps Mary Ellen's, and so many other creators', businesses alive. She adds, "I definitely believe that the entrepreneurial spirit possessed by me and my team is key to our success." There is so much that is given up in pursuit of this dream, and Mary Ellen highlighted the opportunity cost, which all wedding vendors are required to give up. The many hours of working, sacrificed weekends, postponed family plans, and working opposite schedules of your family and friends.

In those moments, working toward something bigger than yourself, believing in your "why" and leaning into your entrepreneurial spirit are what make the long days bearable.

* * *

Hope Taylor introduced and mentioned in the photography chapter and is one of the best examples of a Gen Z entrepreneur I know. Hope started her photography business when she was only seventeen years old when she was in her junior year of high school. Her senior year of high school, she quit her part-time job and went after this dream full-time, despite the mockery of her peers who thought she was being ridiculous. While applying for college, Hope says that something didn't feel right and she was faced with a really tough decision: leave her business completely behind or pursue a degree at a four-year university. She decided instead to chase her dream, revoke her college admission, and pour her heart into growing her business. That was six years ago, and her business is thriving, all because she took a leap of faith and believed in herself.

Entrepreneurship can go beyond your niche focus. Although Hope is mainly a wedding photographer and educator, she also doubles as a social media influencer. Hope mentioned that many photographers and wedding vendors in general are doubling as social media influencers. This takes on many forms, but can include posting about lifestyle, decor, business tips, and more. All while still creating content specific to their niche market. Hope does a phenomenal job at this, giving her followers enough of her personal story and letting us go "behind the scenes" to different aspects of her life, all while maintaining a beautiful Instagram feed and a profession persona. From a business perspective, this is also a great way to help create and maintain a personal brand and help your clients feel more connected to you the business owner. Smartly channeling social media to build a personal brand is a key to thriving as an entrepreneur in this creative field.

Hope and I also chatted about how the wedding industry and wedding vendors are misunderstood. There are so many layers to this questions, but she highlighted some big ones that are prevalent in the industry. Hope says, "A lot of people look at photography or the wedding industry as a whole and believe that it's an easy career choice, that it doesn't take a lot of work or that our prices are too high." Being an entrepreneur in any sense is difficult. You work long days, every day, and you are responsible for promoting yourself. In photography, Hope says that less than ten percent of her job is actually taking photos. The rest involves lots of behind the scenes work, such as editing, marketing, and traveling, which many clients don't realize.

Discussing entrepreneurship with these industry leaders, but especially Hope who is the same age as I am, is so refreshing because so many people, especially in my stage of life just don't "get it." Instead of partying on the weekends, Hope and I are hustling, working on bettering our businesses, ourselves, and looking to help our clients. Hope says she is a huge believer that photography AND business must work together in order to be successful, and I couldn't agree more.

You not only have to be good at what you do, but also you have to be business minded. Typically, it seems people are either creative or analytical, showing more talent in one than the other. Hope says that she LOVES the business side of things, but realizes that most creative-minded people struggle with business and marketing. She has used her love for business and helping others to create courses that teach others how to maximize their business and improve their photography. She educates others by being a conference speaker and teaching online courses, which other photographers and entrepreneurs can sign up to take. This is definitely an unconventional approach to education, but I am very inspired by it and think her approach is helping many people.

Hope's advice for young entrepreneurs truly shows her heart for the industry and for the next generation of girls and women like her who have a dream. She says, "My biggest piece of advice would be to stay true to who you are, but seek knowledge from industry-leading professionals. Attend workshops and conferences, spend hours on YouTube, invest in one-on-one mentoring: learning from the pros is unlike any other form of learning!" No one is going to make your dreams happen except you. People can believe in you, encourage you, and give you advice, but unless you hustle hard and go for it, your dreams will be nothing more than that—dreams. Hope has inspired me so much with her story of working hard, believing in herself, and letting her work speak for itself. And I hope it inspires you too!

* * *

Finally, I want to add how essential it is to surround yourself with a team of like-minded individuals who help push you, inspire you, and encourage you when life is hard. Community is a critical piece regardless of your stage of life. When you have a team with like-minded goals surrounding you, they are there to pick you up on long and difficult days, and you can do the same for them. Brainstorm ideas, set goals, and crush them together. According to *Forbes*, "Letting people take their ideas and see them through is very empowering and motivating. It is a simple component of the entrepreneurial spirit that must remain alive."[137] If you and your team do this, you motivate and empower yourselves, and feel able to achieve more goals and build a

---

137   Smith, Jacquelyn. 2019. "How To Keep Your Entrepreneurial Spirit Alive As The Company You Work For Grows". *Forbes.Com*

bigger business. It's all about consistency and building momentum.

The drive, the grit, and the vision for changing our clients' lives are the fire within us. When days are long and we are tired, that is the motivation that keeps pushing us a little further. We have been entrusted with one of the most important days of someone's life–their wedding day–and we don't take that lightly. So I want to encourage you, regardless of what path you've taken. If you've chosen to pursue your dream as an entrepreneur, you are brave. But if you continue to chase and live this dream without quitting, you are one of the few. A famous quote by Warren G. Tracy's student sums it up the best: "Entrepreneurship is living a few years of your life like most people won't so you can spend the rest of your life like most people can't."[138]

---

138 Silvester, Jessica. 2019. "Start Up – Launch Port – The Open Door Business Blog". *Launch Port - The Open Door Business Blog.*

Chapter 19

Unseen Struggles of Wedding Professionals

I'm sure many wedding vendors feel like I do as I'm writing this: exhausted, slightly frustrated, and wondering if it is really all worth it. I'm working a "double header" event this weekend meaning there was a full-blown one-hundred-person event tonight on Friday, and there will be another one all day tomorrow on Saturday. I'm only awake and writing because I am trying to wear off my caffeine buzz, because I stopped at my favorite drive-through coffee shop at around 5:30 p.m. on the way from my full-time job to this event. And I'm only working that job to support my side-hustle of planning weddings and events.

Now please don't misunderstand me. I'm not writing this for your sympathy or pity. And I know that those of you who are in this field certainly are not going to give it. This is just what we do, and it's what we are used to doing. Working late every weekend, usually Friday, Saturday, and Sunday. Working these twenty to thirty-hour weekends on top of our traditional jobs. Or, if we are so lucky to have this "side job" actually BE our full time livelihood, it eats up just as much of our time and drains us completely. We poured our hearts and souls into these "side-hustles" but when they have grown, we don't know what to do. We don't know how to slow down and take care of ourselves. And I'm reflecting on why?

My first thought is that our society in general struggles with the idea of margin in our lives. Margin is defined by Nourish Media as "the boundaries, the rest that is built into your everyday life, the space between our load and our limits."[139] Margin is the gap that every person needs between rest and exhaustion and is the opposite of complete overload.

However, when someone asks how we are doing, we proudly reply "busy!" as if it's a badge of honor. We rush from job to job, or activity to activity, all while updating social media, squeezing in errands, and making phone calls. Many individuals who work "nine-to-fives" live this lifestyle, and many entrepreneurs chase their

---

139 Schirm, Alexa. 2019. "5 Ways To Create Margin In Life | Nourishedplanner.Com". Nourished Planner.

dreams in the hopes of escaping that ruthless routine. They want to pursue freedom, but in the pursuit, they get lost in the "hustle." Don't get me wrong; it's important to work hard and set goals. But it is also important to have steady control of your life and your schedule and to remember why you started this business in the first place.

Creating margin looks different for everyone, but it can look similar for entrepreneurs. Setting office hours, making a schedule, and sticking to it is absolutely essential. Many people in traditional office jobs or individuals who stay home with their families think that entrepreneurs have plenty of unstructured time and are always available for lunch dates, coffee, or can drop everything and help you run errands or watch your child.

If you are a successful small business owner, especially in the wedding industry, you know that weekdays are not only for recuperating from an exhausting weekend, but also for working relentlessly to prep for the next wedding weekend. Sending emails, making timelines, ordering supplies, drafting contracts and more are just the common things. Not to mention the pressure that now revolves around updating and being highly attentive to social media.

This is another aspect that makes margin and boundaries extremely difficult in this industry. There are so many other talented people that your potential client is reaching out to, the pressure is on to reply immediately. Whether it be at a family dinner, 12 o'clock at night, I know the extreme pressure that awaits. "What if they don't hire me because someone else replied faster?" "It won't take long to send this email." "They booked me and paid me thousands of dollars already-they deserve a reply *right now*." These are the lies we feed ourselves that are ruining our sanity, our clarity, and our margin.

Wedding planning guru Laurie Hartwell reflects on how Generation Z and millennial couples shop for vendors and communicate with wedding professionals. Accessibility is a blessing and a curse for wedding professionals, and couples feel like they have the "right" to Facebook message, Instagram message, or text their photographer or wedding planner at any time of day. Laurie adds, "Because we are so accessible today, I feel that we're losing a piece of ourselves...and we're losing some of our peace. We don't really have much of a personal life anymore, because there's always that on display."

So how do we combat this? It starts with developing and maintaining a healthy relationship with social media. This is the driving force behind businesses and marketing, along with creating perfectly curated websites and automated emails. Putting out authentic content is the first step that reflects your heart and your brand. This will help attract the right kind of people—your "ideal" client.

The next step in creating strong boundaries and having clear communication. Communication begins when you first book a client, telling them your office hours and establishing a certain amount of time they can expect you to reply. If you start a business relationship with healthy boundaries and expectations, it will continue to make the relationship a healthy and enjoyable one that doesn't overwhelm you or make you feel drained.

I think the hardest thing about creating and maintaining boundaries as an entrepreneur is that this is the thing that you've poured your heart and soul into. This is the project or business that you've built from the ground up. And you don't want something to go wrong or clients to stop booking you or for you to get a bad review because of your boundaries. However, I would like to be as bold as to say that you do not deserve to work with people who do not respect your boundaries or do not think that you deserve them. This is something that we need to continue working on, as consumers and as business owners, but I believe this can and will get better as we continue to grow and respect others and ourselves.

Something else that we struggle with, especially in the wedding industry is the concept of opportunity cost. If you aren't familiar with the concept, opportunity cost is defined as "the loss of potential gain from other alternatives when one alternative is chosen"[140] or in simpler language, it is "what you give up when you choose something else." In an everyday example, if you spend your time and money going to a movie with your friends, you cannot spend that same time and money going out to dinner with your significant other. This is a silly example, but I'm sure that just throughout this week you have had to make choices involving opportunity cost. But in the lives of wedding industry entrepreneurs, this hits closer to home.

You get an email from a client scheduling your services eight months from now, on a random Saturday the third weekend of September. You check your calendar, you don't have any other clients booked or conflicts, so you happily email them back with a "yes" and get the process started! The hard part is when its a few weeks before any given event and your best friend calls, says

---

140 "What Does Opportunity Cost Mean?". 2019. *Definitions.Net.*

she's moving, and her last chance to hang out is the weekend of the wedding you have scheduled. Or when your husband's work is throwing him a promotion party and you can't be there because you've already booked a client months in advance. Or when your child is having a piano recital on another Saturday evening for which you already have a commitment.

In my opinion, this is the hardest part of the entire industry. Not truly knowing what's going on in your life or what the future weekends will hold and choosing to selflessly show up and serve your client on the biggest day of their lives, even when part of you wants to be somewhere else.

This is the part that many people don't see. They think you sit around in yoga pants and answer emails during the week, show up on a Saturday to take photos or direct a wedding for a couple of hours, and go home to do the same thing again. It's the tears shed when you have to miss important family events, it's the sixty-plus-hour work weeks you put in, and it's vacations given up and memories that were never made because you choose to honor your commitments and put your business first. It's the opposite work schedules from most people in your life and trying to make time for your partner and family when they work nine to five jobs, and you are working the only time they are off work.

This is why when weekends are full and plans are made and done without you and clients are not booking like you thought they would be, it's hard to carry on and believe that it is truly worth it. However, let me encourage you to keep rekindling that initial spark that made you begin your journey in the first place. Whether it be the pursuit of creativity, the desire to be your own boss, the desire to stay at home with your children more... whatever it is, don't forget it.

Not everyone understands what we do as creative entrepreneurs and what the wedding industry is all about. But it is our job to help them understand. In doing this, it will help give us our boundaries back and help us have more freedom. It will help us be understood and help clients realize how much we are giving up when we commit to serve them, and how much it means to us to be able to do so. This is the path we have forged for ourselves as we keep chasing our dreams and pursuing our vision. Don't lose your "why" in the stressful weekends or in the mundane of checking emails. You have so much to give to the industry and your voice deserves to be heard. You are valuable, creative, and have so much to contribute and so many people to impact.

I'll leave you with this quote. I don't remember where I first heard it, but it was when I was much younger, probably in middle or high school. But it has impacted so much of my personal and entrepreneurial journey and I hope it encourages you too. *"If you have nothing to lose by trying and a great deal to gain if successful, by all means try."*

Acknowledgements

When an opportunity presents itself – I try to always take it. That's how I found myself here. I will be forever grateful for this opportunity as well as the hard lessons it taught me and the person it shaped me into.

When setting out on a long journey you've never embarked on before, you never know how much work it will really take or how long it will be until you reach your final destination. I've learned throughout this journey writing Wedding Z that publishing a book takes an entire community. I am so grateful for all of the support that each person has given me on this journey. Fulfilling this dream would not have been possible without you.

Thank you first and foremost to my family for supporting me through every step of the way. I would not be here without my parents, grandparents, and husband who believed in me and encouraged me to pursue this.

Thank you editors and my New Degree Press family – Eric Koester, Brian Bies, Ashley Alvarez, Cynthia Tucker, and Deanna Drogan. All of you coached me and encouraged me in this process, and kept me on track. I've met every deadline and worked hard knowing I had this team behind me. I wouldn't be here without you.

And thank you to everyone who: gave me their time for a personal interview, pre-ordered the eBook, paperback, and multiple copies to make publishing possible, helped spread the word about *Wedding Z* to gather amazing momentum. Because of you, I am here publishing a book I am proud of. I am sincerely grateful for all of your help.

~Laurie Hartwell	~Hope Taylor	~Mary Ellen LaFreniere
*Roger Decker	Diana Decker	~Melissa Durham
Jannette Hons	Arlene Decker	Shannon Bresnahan
Crystal Hons	Karen Williams	Brenda Gonzalez
Laura Adams-Cooper	Jessica Fuster	Susan Townsend
Kim Shartzer	Rebecca Hott	Marta Y Kastner
Brooke Salitore	Ivy Gaitatzis	Lisa Drogan
Hannah McNulty	John A. Frichtel	Liberty University Dept. of Family & Consumer Sciences

Cindy Grant   Teresa Grant   Mary Ellen Barrett

Alison Pettit   Rachel Beer   Susan Decker

Olivia Martin   Eric Koester   Anastasia Kingsley

Karen Dunn   Hannah Ginion   Isaac Grant

Key:
*multiple copies/campaign contributions,
~featured interviewee

Appendix

Introduction

Claveria, Kelvin. 2019. "Generation Z Statistics: New Report On The Values, Attitudes, And Behaviors Of The Post-Millennials". *Visioncritical.Com.* https://www.visioncritical.com/blog/generation-z-statistics.

Goldberg, Carrie. 2019. "Everything You Need To Know About Priyanka & Nick's Wedding". *Harper's BAZAAR.* https://www.harpersbazaar.com/celebrity/latest/a25107771/priyanka-chopra-nick-jonas-wedding-details/.

Kore, Sakshi. 2019. "Priyanka Chopra And Nick Jonas' Unseen Haldi Pictures". *Vogue India.* https://www.vogue.in/content/priyanka-chopra-and-nick-jonass-unseen-haldi-pictures-are-unmissable.

May, Ashley, and Sean Rossman. 2019. "The Kids Of Gen Z Are Growing Up In A World Far Different Than Their Millennial

Predecessors. So, How Does This Affect Their Thoughts On Love?". *Usatoday.Com*. https://www.usatoday.com/story/news/nation-now/2018/07/09/post-millennial-generation-z-love-dating-marriage-gender-roles/715927002/.

"Nearly Half Of Post-Millennials Are Racial Or Ethnic Minorities". 2019. *Pew Research Center'S Social & Demographic Trends Project*. https://www.pewsocialtrends.org/2018/11/15/early-benchmarks-show-post-millennials-on-track-to-be-most-diverse-best-educated-generation-yet/psdt-11-15-18_postmillennials-00-00/.

Pew Research. 2019. "About Half Of Gen Zers And Millennials Say Same-Sex Marriage, Interracial Marriage Are Good For Society". *Pew Research Center'S Social & Demographic Trends Project*. https://www.pewsocialtrends.org/2019/01/17/generation-z-looks-a-lot-like-millennials-on-key-social-and-political-issues/psdt_1-17-19_generations-09/.

Stevens, Liene. 2019. "2019 State Of The Wedding Industry · Think Splendid®". *Think Splendid®*. https://www.thinksplendid.com/blog/state-of-wedding-industry-2019.

Chapter 1

Head, Tom. 2019. "How Interracial Marriage Laws Have Changed Since The 1600S". *Thoughtco*. https://www.thoughtco.com/interracial-marriage-laws-721611.

Hermanson, Marissa. 2019. "How Millennials Are Redefining Marriage". *The Gottman Institute.* https://www.gottman.com/blog/millennials-redefining-marriage/.

Kagan, Julia. 2019. "Generation X – Gen X". *Investopedia.* https://www.investopedia.com/terms/g/generation-x-genx.asp.

Lakritz, Talia. 2019. "How Marriage Has Changed From Baby Boomers To Millennials". *Insider.* https://www.insider.com/marriage-differences-baby-boomers-millennials-2019-1#most-couples-meet-through-friends-but-more-and-more-millennials-are-meeting-their-significant-others-online-1.

Lebowitz, Shana. 2019. "9 Ways Millennials Are Approaching Marriage Differently From Their Parents". *Business Insider.* https://www.businessinsider.com/how-millennials-gen-x-and-baby-boomers-approach-marriage-2017-11.

Lee, Esther. 2019. "Exclusive: How Gen Z Views Marriage And Weddings—Nearly 90 Percent Plan To Wed Someday". *The Knot News.* https://www.theknotnews.com/exclusive-gen-z-marriage-weddings-37505.

"Online Etymology Dictionary". 2019. *Etymonline.Com.* https://www.etymonline.com/search?q=wed.

Pew Research. 2019. "About Half Of Gen Zers And Millennials Say Same-Sex Marriage, Interracial Marriage Are Good For Society". *Pew Research Center'S Social & Demographic Trends Project*. https://www.pewsocialtrends.org/2019/01/17/generation-z-looks-a-lot-like-millennials-on-key-social-and-political-issues/psdt_1-17-19_generations-09/.

The Holy Bible. 1986. New York: American Bible Society.

Village, Waterloo. 2019. "Wedding Traditions Of The 19Th Century | Partyspace New Jersey". *Partyspace.Com*. https://partyspace.com/newjersey/article/view/wedding-traditions-of-the-19th-century-441.

Chapter 2

None

Chapter 3

Claveria, Kelvin. 2019. "Generation Z Statistics: New Report On The Values, Attitudes, And Behaviors Of The Post-Millennials". *Visioncritical.Com*. https://www.visioncritical.com/blog/generation-z-statistics.

Finch, Jeremy. 2019. "What Is Generation Z, And What Does It Want?". *Fast Company*. https://www.fastcompany.com/3045317/what-is-generation-z-and-what-does-it-want.

Lee, Esther. 2019. "Exclusive: How Gen Z Views Marriage And Weddings—Nearly 90 Percent Plan To Wed Someday". *The Knot News*. https://www.theknotnews.com/exclusive-gen-z-marriage-weddings-37505.

Schawbel, Dan. 2019. "66 Of The Most Interesting Facts About Generation Z". *Danschawbel.Com*. https://danschawbel.com/blog/39-of-the-most-interesting-facts-about-generation-z/#sthash.jQngDH4U.dpuf.

Seemiller, Corey. Ted Talk. 2019. *Generation Z: Making A Difference Their Way*. Video. https://www.youtube.com/watch?v=cNohyudK7nE.

Stevens, Liene. 2019. "2019 State Of The Wedding Industry · Think Splendid®". *Think Splendid®*. https://www.thinksplendid.com/blog/state-of-wedding-industry-2019.

The Knot. "About Us". 2019. *Theknot.Com*. https://www.theknot.com/more/about-us.

Chapter 4

"Definition Of CULTURE". 2019. *Merriam-Webster.Com*. https://www.merriam-webster.com/dictionary/culture.

"Definition Of DIVERSITY". 2019. *Merriam-Webster.Com*. https://www.merriam-webster.com/dictionary/diversity.

Fry, Richard, and Kim Parker. 2019. "'Post-Millennial' Generation On Track To Be Most Diverse, Best-Educated". *Pew Research Center'S Social & Demographic Trends Project*. https://www.pewsocialtrends.org/2018/11/15/early-benchmarks-show-post-millennials-on-track-to-be-most-diverse-best-educated-generation-yet/.

Lamm, Maurice. 2019. "The Jewish Marriage Contract (Ketubah)". *Chabad.Org*. https://www.chabad.org/library/article_cdo/aid/465168/jewish/The-Jewish-Marriage-Contract-Ketubah.htm.

Lo Wang, Hansi. 2019. "Generation Z Is The Most Racially And Ethnically Diverse Yet". *Npr.Org*. https://www.npr.org/2018/11/15/668106376/generation-z-is-the-most-racially-and-ethnically-diverse-yet.

Matthews, Christy, and Michelle Martinez. 2019. "#136 Rituals And Traditions With Author Eleni Gage". Podcast. *The Big Wedding Planning Podcast*. https://www.thebigweddingplanningpodcast.com/rituals-and-traditions.

Maurer, Roy. 2019. "What HR Should Know About Generation Z". *SHRM.* https://www.shrm.org/resourcesandtools/hr-topics/talent-acquisition/pages/what-hr-should-know-about-generation-z.aspx.

Chapter 5

"CGS Survey Reveals 'Sustainability' Is Driving Demand And Customer Loyalty". 2019. *CGS.* https://www.cgsinc.com/en/infographics/CGS-Survey-Reveals-Sustainability-Is-Driving-Demand-and-Customer-Loyalty.

Doan, Dana. 2019. "Community Philanthropy | Learning To Give". *Learningtogive.Org.* https://www.learningtogive.org/resources/community-philanthropy.

Fry, Richard, and Kim Parker. 2019. "'Post-Millennial' Generation On Track To Be Most Diverse, Best-Educated". *Pew Research Center'S Social & Demographic Trends Project.* https://www.pewsocialtrends.org/2018/11/15/early-benchmarks-show-post-millennials-on-track-to-be-most-diverse-best-educated-generation-yet/

Hessekiel, David. 2019. "Engaging Gen Z In Your Social Impact Efforts". *Forbes.Com.* https://www.forbes.com/sites/davidhessekiel/2018/06/26/engaging-gen-z-in-your-social-impact-efforts/#867c12964995.

Chapter 6

Dorsey, Jason. 2019. "Gen Z - Tech Disruption". *Genhq.Com.* https:// genhq.com/wp-content/uploads/2017/01/Research-White-Paper-Gen-Z-Tech-Disruption-c-2016-Center-for-Generational-Kinetics.pdf.

Hebblethwaite, Colm. 2019. "Gen Z Engaging With 10 Hours Of Online Content A Day". *Marketing Tech News.* https://www.marketingtechnews.net/news/2018/feb/09/gen-z-engaging-10-hours-online-content-day/

"Hyperconnected & Collaborative: Gen Z Hits The Workplace". 2019. *Merit Career Development.* http://meritcd.com/blogs/hyperconnected-collaborative-gen-z-hits-the-workplace/.

Kemp, Simon. 2019. "Digital 2019: Global Digital Overview — Datareportal – Global Digital Insights". *Datareportal – Global Digital Insights.* https://datareportal.com/reports/digital-2019-global-digital-overview.

Chapter 7

"Generation Z Craves Experiential Marketing. Here's Why.". 2019. *INPHANTRY.* https://www.inphantry.com/generation-z-craves-experiential-marketing-heres-why/.

Barrett, Jana. 2019. "How To Deliver A Great Customer Experience". *Getfeedback Blog.* https://www.getfeedback.com/blog/great-customer-experience-video/.

Barrows, Sydney. 2019. "Six Ways To Create A Memorable Customer Experience". *Entrepreneur.* https://www.entrepreneur.com/article/206760.

Chapter 8

Glass, Simon, Christopher Wong, David McCarty, and Jane Cheung. 2019. "What Brands Should Know About Generation Z Shoppers". *IBM Institute For Business Value.* https://www.ibm.com/thought-leadership/institute-business-value/report/uniquely-genz.

Kleinschmit, Matt. 2019. "Generation Z Characteristics: 5 Infographics On The Gen Z Lifestyle". *Visioncritical.Com.* https://www.visioncritical.com/blog/generation-z-infographics.

Nichols, Robin. 2019. "Customization And Personalization - Marketing For Millennials". *AB Tasty.* https://www.abtasty.com/blog/customization-and-personalization-two-sides-of-the-same-millennial-coin/.

Wertz, Jia. 2019. "How To Win Over Generation Z, Who Hold $44 Billion Of Buying Power". *Forbes.Com.* https://www.forbes.com/

sites/jiawertz/2018/10/28/how-to-win-over-generation-z-who-hold-44-billion-of-buying-power/#132a180e4c13.

Chapter 9

"10 Questions With Shan-Lyn Ma, Founder & CEO At Zola". 2019. *Medium.* https://medium.com/swlh/10-questions-with-shan-lyn-ma-founder-ceo-at-zola-1af2b762a732.

"About Zola Wedding Registries". 2019. *Zola.* https://www.zola.com/about/index.

Zipkin, Nina. 2019. "Zola Founder Shan-Lyn Ma Shares How To Collaborate And Conquer Your Biggest Challenges". *Entrepreneur.* https://www.entrepreneur.com/article/311589.

"Zola (Company)". 2019. *En.Wikipedia.Org.* https://en.wikipedia.org/wiki/Zola_(company).

Chapter 10

None (all primary interviews)

Chapter 11

None – all primary interviews

Chapter 12

"Anomalie | How To Design A Wedding Dress Online". 2019. *Anomalie*. https://dressanomalie.com/process.

Rosen, Ellen. 2019. "Online Retailers Aim To Shake Up The Wedding Market". *Nytimes.Com*. https://www.nytimes.com/2018/12/19/business/online-retailers-aim-to-shake-up-the-wedding-market.html.

Sweeney, Deborah. 2019. "7 Innovative Entrepreneurs Revolutionizing The Wedding Industry". *Forbes.Com*. https://www.forbes.com/sites/deborahsweeney/2019/04/24/7-innovative-entrepreneurs-revolutionizing-the-wedding-industry/#3df5c9a8cbcb.

"Wedding Dress Cost Guide| Weddingwire". 2019. *Weddingwire*. https://www.weddingwire.com/cost/wedding-dress.

Chapter 13

"Flower Moxie - How Does It All Work". 2019. *Flower Moxie*. https://flowermoxie.com/pages/how-does-it-all-work.

Stevens, Liene. 2019. "2019 State Of The Wedding Industry · Think Splendid®". *Think Splendid®*. https://www.thinksplendid.com/blog/state-of-wedding-industry-2019.

Chapter 14

"Blood & Conflict Diamonds". 2019. *Encyclopedia Britannica*. https://www.britannica.com/topic/blood-diamond.

Chaudhuri, Saikat. 2019. "The Company Bringing Clarity To Online Diamond Shopping". *Mack Institute For Innovation Management*. https://mackinstitute.wharton.upenn.edu/2019/rare-carat-ajay-anand/.

"Conflict Diamond Mining". 2019. *Brilliant Earth*. https://www.brilliantearth.com/conflict-diamond-trade/.

Friedman, Uri. 2019. "How An Ad Campaign Invented The Diamond Engagement Ring". *The Atlantic*. https://www.theatlantic.com/international/archive/2015/02/how-an-ad-campaign-invented-the-diamond-engagement-ring/385376/.

Macon, Alexandra. 2019. "7 Ways Engagement Ring-Buying Is Changing". *Vogue*. https://www.vogue.com/article/how-engagement-ring-buying-is-changing?verso=true.

"Our Story | Couple". 2019. *Couple*. https://couple.co/pages/our-story.

Seemiller, Corey. Ted Talk. 2019. *Generation Z: Making A Difference Their Way*. Video. https://www.youtube.com/watch?v=cNohyudK7nE.

"The History Of Diamond Engagement Rings - American Gem Society". 2019. *Americangemsociety.Org.* https://www.americangemsociety.org/page/diamondasengagement.

Chapter 15

"How It Works". 2019. *Mayflower Venues.* https://www.mayflower-venues.com/how-it-works.

Matthews, Christy, and Michelle Martinez. 2019. "#126 Unique Venues, Unique Perspective: Mayflower Venue's Veronica Armstrong". Podcast. *The Big Wedding Planning Podcast.*

Chapter 16

Anderson, Amy. 2019. "T.D. Jakes: The Instinct To Succeed". *SUCCESS.* https://www.success.com/td-jakes-the-instinct-to-succeed/.

"Definition Of Transparent | Dictionary.Com". 2019. *Www.Dictionary.Com.* https://www.dictionary.com/browse/transparent.

"The Bridal Society - Who We Are". 2019. *Thebridalsociety.Com.* https://www.thebridalsociety.com/about-us.

Chapter 17

None

Chapter 18

"Definition Of ENTREPRENEUR". 2019. *Merriam-Webster.Com*. https://www.merriam-webster.com/dictionary/entrepreneur.

Silvester, Jessica. 2019. "Start Up – Launch Port – The Open Door Business Blog". *Launch Port - The Open Door Business Blog*. https://launchport.wordpress.com/tag/start-up/.

Smith, Jacquelyn. 2019. "How To Keep Your Entrepreneurial Spirit Alive As The Company You Work For Grows". *Forbes.Com*. https://www.forbes.com/sites/jacquelynsmith/2013/10/22/how-to-keep-your-entrepreneurial-spirit-alive-as-the-company-you-work-for-grows/#aed49cac0d40.

Westenberg, Jon. 2019. "Why Now Is The Best Time In Human History To Be An Entrepreneur". *Business Insider*. https://www.businessinsider.com/now-is-the-best-time-to-be-an-entrepreneur-2016-1.

Chapter 19

Schirm, Alexa. 2019. "5 Ways To Create Margin In Life | Nourished-planner.Com". *Nourished Planner*. https://nourishedplanner.com/5-ways-to-create-margin-in-life/.

"What Does Opportunity Cost Mean?". 2019. Definitions.Net. https://www.definitions.net/definition/opportunity+cost.

www.ingramcontent.com/pod-product-compliance
Lightning Source LLC
Chambersburg PA
CBHW071521180526
45171CB00002B/330